PARAGON ISSUES IN PHILOSOPHY

PARAGON ISSUES IN PHILOSOPHY

FORTHCOMING TITLES

THE PARAGON ISSUES IN PHILOSOPHY SERIES

At colleges and universities, interest in the traditional areas of philosophy remains strong. Many new currents flow within them, too, but some of these—the rise of cognitive science, for example, or feminist philosophy—went largely unnoticed in undergraduate philosophy courses until the end of the 1980s. The Paragon Issues in Philosophy Series responds to both perennial and newly influential concerns by bringing together a team of able philosophers to address the fundamental issues in philosophy today and to outline the state of contemporary discussion about them.

More than twenty volumes are scheduled; they are organized into three major categories. The first covers the standard topics—metaphysics, theory of knowledge, ethics, and political philosophy—stressing innovative developments in those disciplines. The second focuses on more specialized but still vital concerns in the philosophies of science, religion, history, sport, and other areas. The third category explores new work that relates philosophy and fields such as feminist criticism, medicine, economics, technology, and literature.

The level of writing is aimed at undergraduate students who have little previous experience studying philosophy. The books provide brief but accurate introductions that appraise the state of the art in their fields and show how the history of thought about their topics developed. Each volume is complete in itself but also complements others in the series.

Traumatic change characterizes these last years of the twentieth century: all of it involves philosophical issues. The editorial staff at Paragon House has worked with us to develop this series. We hope it will encourage the understanding needed in our times, which are as complicated and problematic as they are promising.

John K. Roth   Frederick Sontag
Claremont McKenna College   Pomona College

PHILOSOPHY
AND
COGNITIVE
SCIENCE

ALSO BY JAMES H. FETZER

Author:
Scientific Knowledge: Causation, Explanation, and Corroboration

Artificial Intelligence: Its Scope and Limits

Philosophy of Science (Paragon)

Co-Author:
Glossary of Epistemology/Philosophy of Science (Paragon)

Glossary of Cognitive Science (Paragon)

Editor:
Foundations of Philosophy of Science: Recent Developments (Paragon)

Principles of Philosophical Reasoning

Aspects of Artificial Intelligence

Sociobiology and Epistemology

Epistemology and Cognition

Probability and Causality

Co-Editor:
Program Verification: Fundamental Issues in Computer Science

Philosophy, Language, and Artificial Intelligence

Philosophy, Mind, and Cognitive Inquiry

Definitions and Definability

JAMES H. FETZER
UNIVERSITY OF MINNESOTA, DULUTH

PHILOSOPHY
AND
COGNITIVE
SCIENCE

PARAGON
ISSUES IN
PHILOSOPHY

PARAGON HOUSE · NEW YORK

REVISED EDITION, 1996

PUBLISHED IN THE UNITED STATES BY
PARAGON HOUSE
2700 UNIVERSITY AVENUE WEST
ST. PAUL, MINNESOTA 55114

LIBRARY OF CONGRESS CATALOGING-IN-PUBLICATION DATA

FETZER, JAMES H.
    PHILOSOPHY AND COGNITIVE SCIENCE / JAMES H. FETZER.–2ND ED.
      P.   CM. —(PARAGON ISSUES IN PHILOSOPHY)
    INCLUDES BIBLIOGRAPHICAL REFERENCES AND INDEXES.
    ISBN 1-55778-739-5
    1. PHILOSOPHY AND COGNITIVE SCIENCE. I. TITLE. II. SERIES.
  BF311.F435 1995
  153—DC20
                                                    95-24133
                                                      CIP

MANUFACTURED IN THE UNITED STATES OF AMERICA
10 9 8 7 6 5 4 3 2 1

To
David Smillie

CONTENTS

ACKNOWLEDGMENTS

The cover is a PET (positron emission tomography) scan of a normal human brain that can be technically described as a flurodopa uptake in the basal ganglia of a normal subject (or, in the case of this new edition, as an isometric projection of a transaxial brain slice illustrating decreased metabolic rate for glucose in an abnormal subject). I am grateful to David A. Rottenberg, M.D., Director of the PET Imaging Service of the VA Medical Center in Minneapolis and Professor of Neurology at the University of Minnesota, for his assistance in providing this slide for use.

The work between the covers has been considerably improved because of comments and criticism that I have received from several sources. The suggestions of David Cole, Bret Fetzer, Michael Losonsky, Terry Rankin, and Bill Scott, Jr., are gratefully acknowledged. This would have been a better book had I adopted all their recommendations, but it would also have been a longer one. I have tried to balance issues of content with those of length.

My interest in these questions was kindled by a summer's discussion of gene-culture coevolution with my good friend and former colleague David Smillie. As we appraised the work of Charles Lumsden and E. O. Wilson on human sociobiology, it became increasingly evident that understanding our nature as humans presupposes an adequate account of the nature of mind. I shall always appreciate his gentle encouragement and thoughtful support.

James H. Fetzer

University of Minnesota
Duluth, MN 55812

PREFACE

Cognitive science could be defined as "the science of cognition." This definition would be fine if you already understood both the nature of science and the nature of cognition. In case you don't, this book has been written for you. It provides an introduction to the objectives, characteristics, and methods that tend to distinguish scientific activities from other activities, on the one hand, and to the more specific objectives, characteristics, and methods that differentiate cognitive science from other scientific activities, on the other.

It turns out to be somewhat easier to explain the nature of science than to explain the nature of cognition. The objective of the empirical sciences is to discover those general principles by means of which natural phenomena, including human behavior, might be systematically predicted and explained. These general principles, moreover, have the characteristics of natural laws. A division of labor has emerged within empirical science wherein physicists attempt to discover the laws of physics, chemists the laws of chemistry, and so forth.

This suggests that cognitive scientists attempt to discover natural laws of yet another kind, namely, the laws of cognition. But at just this juncture, a tantalizing difference between this science and those other sciences seems to arise. While there appears to be little room for doubt about the existence of laws of physics, chemistry, and the like, the situation in relation to cognition is another matter altogether. Indeed, among scientists who study human behavior, some even doubt the need for *any* science of cognition at all.

It might therefore be useful to have an introduction to cognitive science that is intended to isolate and identify the principal philosophical difficulties it encounters. Such an introduction would be devoted to discovering why cognitive science is necessary—if it *is* necessary—and even how it is possible— if it *is* possible. This book provides that introduction. It explores the principal problems that cognitive science addresses, the solutions it considers, and the intellectual landscape against which its importance may be measured.

Before turning to this pursuit, something should be said about the relations between three disciplines, which are not always clearly distinguished:

Cognitive Science studies the nature of cognition in human beings, other animals, and inanimate machines (if such a thing is possible). While computers are helpful within cognitive science, they are not essential to its being. A science of cognition could still be pursued even without these machines.

Computer Science studies various kinds of problems and the use of computers to solve them, without concern for the means by which we humans might otherwise resolve them. There could be no computer science if there were no machines of this kind, because they are indispensable to its being.

Artificial Intelligence is a special branch of computer science that investigates the extent to which the mental powers of human beings can be captured by means of machines. There could be cognitive science without artificial intelligence, but there could be no artificial intelligence without cognitive science.

One final caveat: In the case of an emerging new discipline such as cognitive science, there is an almost irresistible temptation to identify the discipline itself (as a field of inquiry) with one of the theories that inspired it (such as the computational conception, which I discuss in Chapter 4). This, however, is a mistake. The field of inquiry (or "domain") stands to specific theories as questions stand to possible answers. The computational conception should properly be viewed as a research program in cognitive science, where "research programs" are answers that continue to attract followers.

The section entitled References lists the authors and titles of the sources that were of special interest to me in the preparation of this book. If you would like to pursue a topic that I discuss but do not know where to begin, take a look and see if something relevant is listed there. The section entitled For Further Reading provides a thumbnail sketch of some other books that offer introductions to cognitive science and closely related disciplines. New books on this topic now appear almost every day.

To summarize: This work provides a philosophical introduction to cognitive science. It is intended to be selective and accessible rather than exhaustive and detailed. I have explored some of the crucial issues that confront this field, rather than attempt to survey every facet of a rapidly growing and increasingly significant area of inquiry. *Philosophy and Cognitive Science* may serve as the text for a first course or as a work to be read on its own. If you discover ways in which it could be improved, please write and let me know. This book is for you.

PREFACE TO 2ND EDITION

The most important difference between this edition and the original is the addition of CHAPTER 2 ARE WE BRAINS IN VATS? Reading a review of the first edition suggested to me that discussion of common-sense ("folk") psychology, of attempts to eliminate the mind in favor of the body, of the idea that we might be brains-in-vats, of different kinds of functionalism and of the motives for moving from folk psychology to cognitive science might be helpful to many students, especially those with no background in the philosophy of mind. It places some crucial issues into perspective.

Moreover, in another review of the first edition, which appeared in the journal *Minds and Machines,* Robert Causey observed that the arguments that I advanced against causal theories of reference in Chapter 3 (now Chapter 4) were not conclusive. Since there appear to be excellent reasons for believing that theories of that kind cannot possibly succeed in achieving their objective, I have reworked my critique to bring out more powerful objections. I have also introduced minor corrections to the text and added a paragraph here and there to clarify my meaning.

While book reviews in professional journals can be very helpful to an author in revising his work, I would like to emphasize a point that I advanced in the Preface to the original edition, namely, that I have written this as an introduction for students and others who want to gain an understanding of cognitive science, which remains one of the most exciting and fastest growing areas of inquiry in the world today. If you find ways in which it could be improved, please write to me and share your thoughts. The capacity for criticism is among our most important traits.

J.H.F.

PHILOSOPHY
AND
COGNITIVE
SCIENCE

CHAPTER ONE

A SCIENCE OF COGNITION

HUMAN BEINGS AS THINKING THINGS

Cognitive science is one of the most active areas of research in the world today. It draws on the combined resources of computer science; artificial intelligence; theoretical linguistics; cognitive, developmental, and evolutionary psychology; and sociobiology. A new discipline with an ancient history, cognitive science is finding new ways to attack old problems, especially by employing scientific techniques to explore questions about the nature of minds as special kinds of systems for processing data, information, and knowledge.

In order to appreciate its importance, it is essential to understand why a science of cognition might matter. What difference would it make, after all, if there were no science of this kind? The answer to this question is likely to be found in the contribution that it can make to understanding ourselves as human beings. René Descartes (1596–1650), an influential French philosopher, suggested that the distinctive feature of human beings is that we are thinking things. A science of cognition might be a science of human nature.

Yet it is not essential to adopt the Cartesian point of view to appreciate the importance of understanding our nature as humans. From a theoretical perspective, human beings are among the most intriguing creatures that evolution has produced. Immense intellectual benefits would accrue from securing a more adequate understanding of the species *Homo sapiens*. And from a practical perspective, the better we understand the causes and the conditions of human behavior, the better we will be able to cope with our fellow humans.

The notion that cognitive science and the explanation of human behavior are intimately intertwined has been artfully expressed by the contemporary cognitive psychologist Jerry Fodor, who has observed that cognitive theories attempt to relate the *intensional properties* of mental states with their *causal capabilities* in affecting behavior (Fodor, 1980, p. 325). Even though it may take a while to appreciate the significance of this position, it hints at a close connection between the theory of cognition and the explanation of behavior.

Although the benefits that we might reap from Fodor's program may be very great, this by itself does not establish that a science of this kind is possible. Whether human beings are thinking things from a philosophical point of view makes a difference from a scientific point of view only so long as our behavior cannot otherwise be predicted and explained. The principle known as "Occam's Razor" even insists that the existence of entities of various kinds (such as minds) ought to be accepted only if it cannot be avoided.

The question therefore arises of whether it might be possible to dispense with the conjecture (or "hypothesis") that human beings are thinking things (i.e. that human beings have minds) from a scientific point of view. For if the behavior of things of this kind could be explained and predicted systematically *without* adopting this hypothesis, then surely it should be set off to one side as a flight of philosophical fancy lacking the scientific significance that would enable it to qualify as something more than merely idle speculation.

There is even a name for the view that mental phenomena—ideas and thoughts, dreams and daydreams, conjectures and speculations, for example—are nothing more than incidental by-products of the causal processes that themselves determine the behavior of human beings. This position is referred to by the imposing title of *epiphenomenalism*. Hence, if mental phenomena are epiphenomena, they have no role to play in the causation of human behavior. If this were true, the point of cognitive science would be obscure.

The first challenge encountered in considering the prospects for a science of cognition thus appears to be establishing whether this activity is required at all! One source of support for adopting the epiphenomenal position would be to maintain that brain processes preempt mental processes. If our brain rather than our mind causes our behavior—if behavior is caused by neurons rather than by beliefs, for example—cognitive science may be something we can live without. So if cognitive science is not dispensable, how can we tell?

The answer to this question, like the answers to many other questions we shall consider, may be much more subject to debate than we might desire. The adequacy of a theoretical position on an issue of this kind tends to be a function of its relative plausibility in comparison with alternative positions. The argument that I shall offer suggests that cognitive science is indispensable because mental states fulfill an essential role in scientific explanations of behavior. The argument is not conclusive, and it takes time to develop.

EXPLAINING HUMAN BEHAVIOR

The possible explanations available for human behavior are abundant and diverse. To assess the scientific standing of a hypothesis (or "theory"), however, it is first necessary to specify those characteristics that are supposed to contribute to its scientific status. As an *ad hoc* measure, let us assume that any theory that properly qualifies as "scientific" must have the properties of being conditional, testable, and tentative. We shall attempt to refine this conception later on. But let us now consider the following theories or hypotheses, beginning with (H1):

(H1) The God Theory. God brings all things to pass.

This hypothesis is not conditional, because it does not specify the conditions relative to which behavior of one kind rather than another would occur. It is also not testable, because it is compatible with any possible course of human behavior. No matter what happens, it could be explained by appealing to this theory. And it is not tentative, because there are no evidential conditions under which an adherent would be rationally required to abandon (H1). It is therefore not scientific and would render cognitive science dispensable, in principle, unless God relies upon our mental states to attain his own ends.

In rendering this assessment, I have assumed that the name "God" stands for the traditional monotheistic conception of an omniscient, omnipotent, and benevolent deity. There is no special reason for making this assumption, except that *some* interpretation of its meaning is required. Notice, in particular, that if the thing named by that name were to change, the scientific standing of that hypothesis would change with it. Were "God" the name of some individual dog ("god" spelled backward), for example, it would then be both testable and false.

(H2) The Chance Theory. Everything happens by chance.

This hypothesis suggests that there are no reasons why human beings might behave one way rather than another under different circumstances. It does not specify those conditions, precisely because it asserts that they make no difference. If evidence that there are such conditions is taken to undermine this theory, then it is testable (albeit indirectly) and tentative, because that same evidence tends to suggest that (H2) is false and should be abandoned. If it were true, it would likewise suggest that cognitive science is unneeded.

The chance theory must not be confused with a probabilistic theory that assigns specific probability values to different possible outcomes that might occur under specific conditions. The hypothesis that I like Rocky Road more than twice as much as I like Heavenly Hash, for example, suggests that I will choose Rocky Road more than twice as often as I choose Heavenly Hash when we visit Baskin Robbins. This hypothesis is conditional, testable, and should be viewed as tentative— my preference for ice cream flavors might change!

The idea that a theory should be "tentative" can be interpreted in several different ways. Since a preference for ice cream (fast cars, loud music, etc.) is a property that can change, it is certainly true that a theory about a person's preferences should be tentative *because* of its subject matter. But there is a deeper sense in which a theory should be tentative *regardless* of its subject matter, namely, our confidence in the truth of a theory should depend upon and vary with the available relevant evidence. This is the crucial sense here.

(H3) The Homunculus Theory. There is a little person in each human head.

This hypothesis shifts attention from us to the little people inside of us as directors of our behavior. No matter what behavior we may display, it can be explained by appealing to our homunculus. If X-rays, heat scans, and such are permissible methods for detecting the presence or absence of these little people, the theory is testable, tentative, and probably false. Nonetheless, its most striking feature is its failure to explain the behavior of the homunculi. The only cognitive science that hypothesis (H3) supports is for little people.

The homunculus theory affords a vivid illustration of a special kind of problem that explanations can encounter. It may appear to be problematic because it has the character of a regressive explanation, which "passes the buck" to some earlier event, previous cause, etc., which "passes the buck" again to some earlier event, previous cause, etc., in turn. This is normally a problem only when the earlier event, previous cause, etc., itself is not understood. One billiard ball hitting another, hitting another, . . . in a chain reaction is not problematic, but the idea of ever smaller homunculi-within-homunculi is.

EXPLANATIONS WITHOUT COGNITION

None of these theories supports cognitive science and none of these theories is scientific, which may create the impression that they do not support cognitive science *because* they are not scientific. It might therefore be useful to consider some additional alternative explanations of human behavior that qualify as *scientific* (according to our standards) but nevertheless offer no support for cognitive explanations. While the first of these might seem to be somewhat simpleminded, the second is of a very sophisticated kind.

(H4) The Soma-Type Theory. An individual's personality varies with his (or her) body type:

> Endomorphs tend to be vicerotonic.
> Mesomorphs tend to be somatonic.
> Ectomorphs tend to be cerebrotonic.
> Etc.

So long as these body types (endomorphic, mesomorphic, ectomorphic, etc.) and personality profiles (vicerotonic, somatonic, cerebrotonic, etc.) are sufficiently clearly delineated to permit the presence or the absence of the properties thereby defined to be directly or indirectly ascertained by means of observation or measurement, this theory satisfies the requirements of being conditional, testable, and tentative. It makes no appeal to cognitive states, however, and therefore does not support the necessity for cognitive science.

Without knowing the meaning of the technical terms that occur within the context of this theory, it would be impossible to even guess what kinds of information—what observations, measurements, or experiments—might be appropriate to gather evidence relevant for assessing its truth or falsity. Once those terms are understood by means of more familiar language, we have:

(H4) The Soma-Type Theory. An individual's personality varies with his (or her) body type:

> Thick-bodied people tend to be extroverted.
> Broad-bodied people tend to be athletic.
> Thin-bodied people tend to be introverted.
> Etc.

The kind of evidence that would be relevant no longer seems mysterious.

The use of the phrase "tend to be" does make these hypotheses somewhat more vague than would be the case if they specified the strengths of those tendencies. If *all* endomorphs are supposed to be vicerotonic with no exceptions, for example, the discovery of even *one* endomorph that is not vicerotonic would be conclusive evidence that hypothesis (H4) is false. But the certainty with which that could be established would tend to vary with the certainty with which something could be said to be "endomorphic," etc.

(H5) The Behaviorist's Theory. An individual organism's behavior can be systematically predicted on the basis of knowledge of the kind of organism that that individual happens to be and the history of reinforcement to which it has been sub-

jected, which yields a probability of response for specific behavior under specific conditions.

As with many others, this theory can be refined to take into account differences between species, between types of histories of reinforcement, and between probabilities of response for various kinds of behavior under various stimulus conditions. It appears to satisfy the desiderata of being conditional, testable, and tentative. Most strikingly, it represents a position that has been widely embraced by serious students of human and of animal behavior. Its scientific credentials are difficult to deny, yet it leaves no place for cognition.

Indeed, in the hands of the influential behaviorist, B. F. Skinner, this position has served as a virtual bedrock of opposition to cognitive psychology. He maintains that reference to inner mental states of an organism is never indispensable, because the behavior caused by those inner states can be inferred directly from the histories of reinforcement that brought them about (Skinner 1953). The argumentative strategy that Skinner has employed thus assumes more or less the following form: If A causes B and B causes C, then even though A does not directly cause C, the predictive inference from A to C is justifiable.

Skinner advances his position in the name of scientific methodology. He wants to eliminate the use of language that refers to theoretical or unobservable properties—in this case, mental states—because he thinks that the use of language of this kind is *unscientific*. Thus, if links can be established between the values of observable variables—such as an organism's species and history of reinforcement A relative to its subsequent behavior C—that is all that science requires. Even if intermediate links via theoreticals such as B are helpful in establishing connections between observables such as A and C, once those links have been established, reference to B is no longer required.

This argument, which Carl G. Hempel, an important contemporary philosopher of science, has dubbed "the theoretician's dilemma," is entirely general in its significance. Suppose, for example, that ordinary mental states of human beings (including, especially, motives and beliefs) were produced by our environmental histories, where those states are stored in our neural networks. Even if our behavior were directly caused by interaction between our mental states and environmental stimuli, the predictive inferences that could be drawn from our histories to our subsequent behavior would still be valid.

Since this argument lends great weight to the conclusion that cognitive science is dispensable, after all, it should come as a considerable relief that the theoretician's dilemma cannot be sustained for at least four important reasons (for his technical discussion, see Hempel, 1965, esp. pp. 220–22).

First, it denies the systematic role performed by positing the existence of cognitive states, each of which has no end of causal manifestations under varied test conditions. (Ask yourself how you could exhaust the potential causal consequences of, say, your belief that you live at a specific address.)

Second, it ignores the possibility that even indirect knowledge of these inner cognitive states may be more readily accessible than any knowledge of the histories that induced them. (Indeed, we ordinarily infer that someone is in a certain belief state without knowing how they came to be in it.)

Third, it overlooks the requirement that an adequate explanation must take into account each factor whose presence or absence made a difference to the behavior to be explained. (Notice, especially, that once a probability of response has been acquired, its history of acquisition no longer matters.)

Finally, it disregards the consideration that, without access to premises that relate cause A to effect B and cause B to effect C, it would be impossible to derive the predictive inference from A to C. (This means that even Skinner could not secure his own conclusion without positing these inner states.)

COGNITION AND EXPLANATION

The theoretician's dilemma represents one version of a movement that is known as *reductionism*. In Skinner's case, the reductionistic aspect is to dispense with theoretical language (describing inner mental states that are not accessible to direct observation and measurement) in favor of exclusively observational language (describing publicly observable stimuli and publicly observable responses). Within its historical context, Skinner's aversion to theoretical language represented a reaction to the excesses of an earlier time when consciousness was the subject and introspection was the method.

In relation to the subjective psychology of consciousness elaborated, for example, by William James (1842–1910), the objective psychology of behavior that J. B. Watson (1878–1958) advocated and Skinner adopted was welcome news, indeed. But the positive benefits that initially attended this corrective reaction gradually deteriorated into a reactionary posture unable to contend with new ways of thinking about the nature of meaning and mind. The possibility of cognitive science was ruled out on methodological grounds, as though explanatory relevance were simply a matter of public accessibility.

The problem appears to have been an overly strict construction of scientific objectivity. However plausible it may seem to be to associate scientific objectivity with public accessibility, the conditions imposed by science in relation to empirical testability only require *intersubjective reliability* instead. This means that any scientist confronted by the same relevant evidence, the same theoretical alternatives, and relying upon the same principles of logic, would arrive at the same tentative conclusions. It does not demand that the only evidence that qualifies as scientific must be open to direct observation.

Indeed, the straitjacket that such rigid requirements would impose does not appear to be justifiable even in the spirit in which they were advanced. While *logical positivism*, the dominant philosophy of science of the first half of the twentieth century, held that theoretical hypotheses, in principle, should be reducible to finite sets of observation sentences, that view cannot be reconciled with the realization that even reports of observations turn out to be "theory laden." Even ordinary language appears to be highly theoretical.

You might think, for example, that describing something as, say, *a glass of water*, makes use of purely observational language. But when we describe something as "water", we attribute to it many different properties, including that it would tend to quench our thirst if we were to drink it, that it might help in putting out a fire if we were to pour it on one, that it could be heated to a boil and be used for cooking, and so on. These are theoretical properties implied by describing the contents as "water". If you have any doubt about this, consider your expectations if it had been described as "alcohol" instead.

The adoption of excessive requirements of objectivity would be enough to doom the prospects for any science of cognition, precisely because inner mental states are not accessible to public observation. The adoption of an unjustifiable conception of scientific methodology, it thus turns out, would completely preclude the theoretical possibility of *any* science of cognition. A theory that could not satisfy the restrictions that Skinner would impose indicates the possibilities permitted by more liberal conceptions of science; for example:

(H6) Genetic Epistemology. There are four stages in each person's intellectual development (Ginsburg and Opper, 1969):

> the sensorimotor stage (0 to 2 years);
> the preoperational stage (2 to 7 years);
> the concrete operational stage (7 to 11 years); and,
> the formal operational stage (11 years on up).

So long as the presence or the absence of each of these stages is directly or indirectly accessible to empirical determination (by means of observations and inferences based upon them), this theory, which is related to the work of the Swiss psychologist and philosopher Jean Piaget (1896–1980), seems to qualify as conditional, testable, and tentative. What is most important about this example for our purposes, therefore, is that it represents a scientific theory concerning stages in the development of cognitive abilities.

The testability of this theory appears fairly obvious, because it implies that a person z of a specific age will be at a specific stage of development:

(H6) Genetic Epistemology. There are four stages in each person's intellectual development:

> if a person z is between 0 and 2, then z is at the sensori-motor stage;
> if a person z is between 2 and 7, then z is at the preoperational stage;
> if a person z is between 7 and 11, then z is at the concrete operational stage; and,
> if a person z is older than 11, then z is at the formal operational stage.

Since these hypotheses are supposed to be true of any person, z, at all, they have the (implicit) form of what are known as *universal generalizations*, which assert that everything of a specific kind has a certain attribute. A universal generalization is false if even one instance of its reference property (a person between 0 and 2) lacks the attribute (sensorimotor stage).

As you may already realize, to test this theory it would be essential to know at least some of the behavioral manifestations characteristic of each of these stages of cognitive development. It would also be indispensable to have information about the ages of any test subjects. Whenever some level of development (say, a process of "decentration" during which a child begins to separate himself from his environment) is associated with a specific age, the behavior that is symptomatic of that level has to be explicitly specified.

SCIENTIFIC THEORIES AND LAWS

The soma-type theory (H4), the behaviorist's theory (H5), and genetic epistemology (H6) can be compared with respect to temporal parameters. (H4) specifies relations between body type and personality profile that are contemporaneous (in other words, they are supposed to be properties that are present simultaneously). (H5) specifies relations between an organism's behavior at a time t (in the present, let us say) and the history of reinforcement it has endured at times previous to t (during the past). (H6), however, specifies a fixed sequence of stages in the cognitive development of every individual across specific intervals during their lifetime.

In spite of their differences, these theories are reasonable candidates for empirical investigation, precisely because they appear to possess the features required of scientific theories. Indeed, Hempel (1965, p. 117) suggests that the relative adequacy of theories might best be envisioned as a matter of degree and assessed relative to multiple criteria, including:

(a) the clarity and precision of the language in which they are expressed;

(b) the systematic (i.e. explanatory and predictive) power that they yield;

(c) the elegance with which they attain that measure of systematic power; and

(d) the extent to which they have been confirmed by empirical inquiries.

Since systematic power implies conditionality and confirmability implies testability and tentativeness, (a)–(d) support the standards we have used.

One crucial aspect about scientific explanations has yet to be addressed, since the relations between reference and attribute properties with which a theory deals have to be of a special kind. In particular, for sentences ascribing personality types to body types, probabilities of response to different histories of reinforcement, or stages of intellectual development to individuals of different ages to qualify as *lawlike sentences* (i.e. as sentences that would be laws of nature if they were true), they must concern what we will call permanent-property rather than mere transient-property relations.

At least three different ways in which something of kind R might have an attribute of kind A need to be distinguished. The first occurs whenever the attribute A is a property of every instance of reference property R as a function of our language. The second occurs whenever attribute A is something that one or more instances of property R happens to have as transient properties. The third occurs whenever attribute A is something that every instance of property R must have because A is a permanent property of R.

These distinctions sound more complicated than they really are. If you were asked to explain why freshmen are students (why Ferraris are automobiles, etc.), it would not be difficult for you to do. You would simply explain that the word "freshmen" means students in their first year of studies (that "Ferrari" is the name of an expensive sports car, etc.). In doing so, you would have appealed to the fact that these attributes are properties of anything of those kinds as a function of the definition of words in our language.

Such explanations may be viewed as trivial but true. If you were asked to explain why every teenager wears T-shirts (why every Ferrari is painted red, etc.), that would be more difficult. There are no invariable reasons why someone wears a T-shirt (why a car is painted red, etc.). Attributes such as these are merely transient properties that something of the kind *teenager* (*Ferrari*, etc.) could gain or lose while remaining a thing of that kind. Things of those kinds have transient properties in common merely by coincidence.

A specific personality type would be a permanent property of a specific body type, by contrast, if there were no processes or procedures, natural or contrived, by means of which that personality type could be separated from that body type without losing that body type as well. In other words, even though it is no part of the meaning of "endomorph" (where endomorphs are thick-bodied) that endomorphs have to be vicerotonic (where vicerotonics are sociable and outgoing), it should be impossible to lose that personality type when of that body type, if this actually qualifies as a natural law.

A comparison with chemistry may be instructive here. It is not part of the definition of "gold" that everything that is gold has the melting point of 1063° C. According to the periodic table of the elements, by means of which stuff that is gold is defined, those things are gold whose atoms have atomic number 79 (a function of the number of protons in the nucleus of an atom of that kind). Relative to this reference property, everything gold has the same melting point, which does not vary from time to time or from place to place, given that this relationship does in fact represent a law of nature.

A crucial difference between relations of these kinds is that the presence of a permanent attribute can be explained by subsuming it as an instance of some corresponding (true) natural law, whereas the presence of a transient attribute cannot. Sometimes, however, it may be very hard to discern which is which. The comedic talents of a Jackie Gleason, Jonathan Winters, or John Belushi could be explained by reference to the generalization that endomorphs are vicerotonic (colloquially, that fat men are jolly) if that generalization is both lawlike and true, but not if this is just accidental.

This reflection raises the possibility that the method of conjectures and (attempted) refutations, which Sir Karl Popper has proposed as essential to empirical science, may fulfill a role within cognitive science similar to that it plays in other scientific domains. Lawlike hypotheses can be tested by trying to refute them. If it were possible to create or to discover endomorphs who are not vicerotonic (gold lumps that do not have the melting point of 1063° C, etc.), that would establish conclusive evidence that those theories were not true. Sincere but unsuccessful attempts to refute them, moreover, can provide evidence in their support, which suggests they might be true.

This Popperian methodology of "corroboration" thus requires that the positive significance of *unsuccessful* attempts to falsify a hypothesis has to be taken into account along with the negative significance of *successful* attempts to falsify that hypothesis. Otherwise, it would be impossible to possess appropriate grounds for preferring one hypothesis over another, since the evidence available is always insufficient to guarantee that the truth—about the world and ourselves—has in fact ever been ascertained.

These distinctions provide assurance that the very idea of a science of cognition is not fundamentally misconceived. One argument that we have considered, however, has yet to receive its proper disposition. For, if explanations in terms of brain states take precedence over explanations in terms of mind states, then perhaps cognitive science, although possible, is not necessary, after all. It is striking to realize that each of the arguments that applied to Skinner's position apply here with equal force.

First, the systematic power of explanations by means of mental states has to be retained by any explanations in terms of brain states. (Any loss of systematic power would mean that mental-state explanations cannot be replaced by brain-state explanations without simply changing the subject.)

Second, our inferential knowledge of mental states is ordinarily more accessible and more reliable than the information that one might possess about someone's brain state. (Even in cases of intoxication or brain damage, the inference that something physical is wrong involves indirect reasoning.)

Third, the contributions of mental states to behavior are independent of the specific brain states to which they may be related. (Notice, in particular, that the explanatory power of mental states remains intact even if they can be properties of more than one—possibly numerous—brain states.)

Fourth, without access to information that relates brain states to mind states, on the one hand, and mind states to their behavioral effects, on the other, it would be impossible to derive any predictive inference from brain states to behavioral effects. (So mind states are not dispensable, after all!)

I would admit that, in one additional respect, the situation does appear to be more cloudy. It is difficult to imagine that brain states are no longer explanatorily relevant in relation to corresponding mind states, especially when those mind states are taken to be permanent properties of those brain states. This means, after all, that it is contrary to the laws of nature (relating mind states and brain states) to lose a mind state without also losing a related brain state, even though the presence of that mind state is not part of what it means to be in that brain state. The difficulty that arises in contending with this issue, however, appears to result from the existence of laws of several different kinds, a matter that we shall explore in Chapter 6.

The parallel critiques of these positions should not be especially surprising, because, as specific instances of reductionism applied within the philosophy of mind, they are but special cases of the theoretician's dilemma. Any arguments that succeed in resolving that dilemma should hold against these instances. Neither the behavioristic reduction (of theoretical to observational language) nor the physicalistic reduction (of mental states to brain states) appears to be rationally warranted. The results of this chapter thus suggest that a science of cognition is both necessary and possible, which is a welcome inference. If it's not, you should stop reading this book right now!

CHAPTER TWO

ARE WE BRAINS IN VATS?

COMMON-SENSE PSYCHOLOGY

Before turning to the basic concepts of cognitive science, it might be worthwhile to consider the background against which this discipline has emerged. This includes what is known as common-sense (or "folk") psychology among popular beliefs and "eliminative materialism" among philosophical analyses. We shall also have occasion to consider one of the most intriguing ideas that human imagination has produced, namely, the possibility that we might be nothing more than brains in vats. This conjecture will lead to a distinction between two kinds of *functionalism*, which, in turn, supplies a foundation for differentiating between at least three distinct conceptions of cognition.

Common-sense (or "folk") psychology may be identified as the kind of psychology that most of us attribute to ourselves and to others in attempting to explain and to predict our behavior. As a first approximation, it is the psychology of *beliefs* and *desires*, which holds that human behavior is brought about (or "caused") by the interaction of our motives and beliefs. (For discussions, see Louch (1966) and Care and Landesman, eds. (1968).) If someone were to ask you why you are reading this book, for example, you might respond by telling them that you want to learn about the character of cognitive science. This reply combines an assertion regarding your motive for reading it with an implied belief about the contents of this book.

Other cases, however, suggest that motives and beliefs are

not enough to account for our activities. Suppose, for example, that a friend of yours happened to be asked why she has never read *Fanny Hill*, an erotic novel which dates from Victorian times about the adventures of a young woman. It would not be surprising to learn, by way of response, that she does not read books of that kind because she considers them to be "immoral". Indeed, there are many kinds of activities in which we do not engage on the ground that it violates our sense of morality or what we take to be proper.

Most of us, for example, know that money can be made in a variety of different ways, including getting a job, robbing banks, and counterfeiting credit cards. Most of us also want to make money. We therefore possess a combination of motives and beliefs that might lead many of us into activities of such kinds, were they the only factors influencing our behavior. For most of us, however, robbing banks and counterfeiting credit cards are simply not among our available options. We exclude from consideration those kinds of behavior that we rule out on ethical or moral grounds.

A more adequate account of common-sense (or "folk") psychology, in other words, would take *ethics* into account as well, yielding explanations of behavior based upon combinations of motives, beliefs and ethics. Yet even that broader conception does not appear to be sufficient to capture common-sense psychology. We do not expect those who do not know the English language (how to play tennis, read Braille and so on), for example, to engage in activities of that kind. We take for granted that, in order to understand human behavior, we must consider individual *abilities* as well.

Even those who possess corresponding abilities, however, may or may not be in a position to exercise them. When a friend who speaks English, for example, is incapacitated from exercising that ability (because he is bound and gagged), we exonerate him from responsibility for failing to do something (warning us of the presence of a burglar in the house, say) that he otherwise would have done. The kind of exercise of abilities we ordinarily expect to occur, it appears, can be affected by the influence of countervailing factors that inhibit their exercise, including, for example, being intoxicated, unconscious, brain-damaged or otherwise constrained.

A (more or less) complete reconstruction of common-sense (or "folk") psychology, therefore, would take into account not only the motives and beliefs that affect our behavior but also our morals, our abilities and our capabilities. Indeed, it does not appear to be far-fetched to imagine that, in ordinary life and daily conversations, we typically tend to explain and to predict the behavior that we and others display on the basis of assumptions about causal interactions between the motives, the beliefs, the ethics, the abilities and the capabilities that we ascribe to others and to ourselves.

From this perspective, at least three features of common-sense psychology deserve consideration. The first is that "folk" psychology appears to be chock-full of *subjunctive conditionals* (about what individuals could, would or should do, regarding the future) and *counterfactual conditionals* (about what individuals could have done, would have done or should have done, concerning the past). The terms that are used to name these conditionals may sound unfamiliar to you, but ask yourself how much of your conversations about people could be conducted without using language of this kind.

The second is that common-sense psychology appeals to combinations of motives, beliefs, ethics, abilities and capabilities to explain our behavior, yet, *on its own*, does not explain why we succeed when we succeed or why we fail when we fail. We may act on our beliefs (such as that Bob is a good friend, someone we can trust with our secrets), but later discover we were mistaken (when he betrays our confidence). Our successes and failures in life—apart from the influence of luck—are largely determined by the extent to which the world *is* the way we take it to be—by the extent to which our beliefs are true. This reflects the reality of the *opportunities* we confront.

The third is that, even when we take into account everything that we take to be relevant to a particular action by a specific person (such as Jill's arriving at a decision on whether to marry Jack), we appear to leave room for at least two kinds of uncertainty. One is that we may have left out relevant conditions simply because we are unaware of them (such as that Jack does not like her mother, which matters to Jill). The other is that the action itself might be the outcome of a probabilistic process, where sometimes one result (getting married) occurs, sometimes another (remaining single), under the same relevant conditions. Some decisions might be like flips with a coin.

ELIMINATIVE MATERIALISM

The conception of common-sense (or "folk") psychology that has been offered here appears to receive considerable confirmation in relation to the conversations we have everyday about the behavior of persons with whom we are acquainted and others with whom we are not. No doubt, a large measure of our fascination with the foibles and crimes committed by our fellow human beings is figuring out (what we take to be) how they ever got into those predicaments in the first place. That includes our interest, for example, in Amy and Joey, Tonya and Nancy, the Menendez brothers, and O. J., Ron and Nicole. We want to know *how* and *why* what happened happened.

Common-sense psychology thus seems to fare well in relation to one of the multiple criteria of theoretical adequacy, namely, the extent to which it has been confirmed by empirical inquiries. This finding does not settle the question, however, because "folk" psychology does not fare equally well relative to others. The language of motives, beliefs, ethics, abilities, and capabilities in which "folk" psychology is expressed, for example, also appears to be somewhat vague and imprecise. When we describe someone, say, as "excited" or as "depressed", what we mean may or may not correspond to what others may mean when they use the same language.

This should come as no surprise if the vast majority of us happen to use language in ways that differ in grammar and vocabulary—sometimes significantly, but often not—from one another. We still tend to share an overlapping common core that, by and large, enables us to communicate successfully with other members of our community. One way to tell whether or not we mean the same thing by the words we use is whether we tend to classify the same cases the same way. When we classify the same cases as cases of *excitement* and of *depression*, for example, that tends to support the inference that we are using similar language in similar ways.

If the language of common-sense psychology is vague and imprecise, however, then we have to consider the possibility that the reason why it appears so well-confirmed is because it is vague and ambiguous. Unless we are considering something that properly qualifies as *the same theory*, after all, we may be confirming various members of *a family of theories*, where there could be as many theories as there are people holding them. This makes it even more important to observe that the explanatory and predictive power of "folk" psychology appears to be generally confined to relatively ordinary behavior by persons who are physiologically normal.

Cases in which persons are brain-damaged or otherwise neurologically impaired, for example, tend to fall beyond the scope of application of common-sense psychology. Persons whose motives, beliefs, ethics, abilities or capabilities deviate significantly from the norm—who suffer from serious mental derangement, for example—are largely inexplicable on the basis of common-sense psychology. Part of our fascination with a Charles Manson, a John Gacy or a Jeffrey Dahmer, say, derives from the implicit realization that their behavior is deviant enough to be inexplicable to common-sense.

Another problem that confronts common-sense psychology is that the explanations that it does supply appear to explain *behavior* by means of *tendencies toward behavior*, which (upon initial consideration, at least) may make it seem to be circular. When a person *acts* jealous (hostile, insincere, etc.), we tend to explain their behavior by inferring that they *are* jealous (hostile, insincere, etc.). These tendencies toward behavior generally assume the form of *dispositions*, understood as characteristic ways of behaving under certain specifiable conditions. A wife-beater, for example, tends to beat his wife when he becomes angry, jealous, insecure and such.

One way in which problems of vagueness and imprecision and of seeming circularity might be suitably resolved would be the adoption of (what appears to be) a more scientific approach by attempting to find the brain states that underlie these mental states. In other words, if jealousy (hostility, insincerity, etc.) are indeed dispositions to behave in characteristic ways under certain specifiable conditions, then perhaps a rigorous science of human behavior might be developed by searching for and discovering underlying brain states. The successful discovery of these brain states, however, might either not support or even undermine "folk" psychology itself.

Paul Churchland, an ardent advocate of this position, which is known as *eliminative materialism*, for example, holds that folk psychology is not merely incomplete but is also inaccurate as a "*mis*representation" of our internal states and mental activities. He therefore contends that the progress of neuroscience should lead not to the reduction of folk psychology to neuroscience but to its wholesale elimination (Churchland, 1984, p. 43). The model Churchland endorses is analogous to the elimination of *phlogiston* from vocabulary of chemistry and the elimination of *witches* from the vocabulary of human typology, where he thinks the categories of *motives, beliefs* and such are destined for the same fate as neuroscience develops.

Churchland admits that he can provide no guarantee that

the development of neuroscience must produce the elimination of folk psychology in its wake. The situation might turn out to be far less drastic, perhaps requiring the elimination of a few folk-psychological concepts or the adjustment of a few folk-psychological principles. He therefore allows that the position he represents might be better described as "revisionary materialism" than as "eliminative materialism". And, indeed, given the extent to which we interact with one another on a daily basis, it does appear difficult to accept the notion that folk psychology should be entirely mistaken.

MINDS AS BRAINS IN VATS

The deeper problem that confronts eliminative materialism, however, seems to be the same problem confronting classic forms of reductionism, namely, that without access to information relating brain states to mind states, on the one hand, and mind states to behavioral effects, on the other, it would be impossible to derive any predictive inference from brain states to behavioral effects. And if those behavioral effects are manifestations of dispositions toward behavior under specific conditions, it appears unlikely that a "mature" neuroscience could accomplish its goals if it lacked the capacity to relate brain states to behavioral effects by way of dispositions.

In the case of jealousy (hostility, insincerity, etc.), after all, if we want to discover the brain states that underlie these mind states, which are understood as dispositions toward behavior under specific conditions, then a rigorous science of human behavior might be developed by searching for and discovering underlying brain states, where those dispositions toward behavior are appropriately (presumably, *lawfully*) related to those brain states. The discovery of brain states that were not appropriately related to corresponding mind states would be pointless neuroscience.

It would be unsurprising, however, if folk-psychological

language had to be made more uniform and precise in order to attain a greater degree of scientific significance or if its scope of application could only be expanded by taking into account successively more and more abnormal (or "borderline") cases. Indeed, theory construction in psychology appears to represent an approach of this kind, where various types of abnormal personality are defined by language that relates them to (more or less) ordinary folk-psychological categories. The *Diagnostic and Statistical Manual of the American Psychological Association* (DSM-IV) supplies many illustrations.

From this perspective, Churchland's model of the future elimination of the categories of motives and beliefs as analogous to the elimination of the category of witches appears to be misconceived. Indeed, the category of witches was reserved for certain kinds of cases that were supposed to be instances of *abnormal* motives, beliefs, abilities and such. Witches were people who could do things—cast spells, communicate with spirits, raise the dead and the like—that were beyond the scope of ordinary abilities. The elimination of witches from the category of possible combinations of human attributes appears to be merely an adjustment to folk psychology.

A less-faulty analogy could be readily drawn from the history of chemistry in relation to the development of the atomic theory of matter. In the past, for example, "gold" was defined as a yellow, malleable metal with a melting point of 1063° C, a boiling point of 2600° C, which is ductile and very malleable, etc. The development of the atomic theory of matter permitted the redefinition of "gold" as the element with atomic number 79, relative to which the properties of being a yellow malleable metal with a melting point of 1063° C, a boiling point of 2600° C and so forth were now related by law rather than by definition. This was a considerable advance.

Indeed, the analogy with human behavior appears to be well-founded. The properties of things that are *gold* (such as melting points and boiling points) are dispositions toward behavior under specific conditions just as are those of things that are *human* (including jealousy, hostility and insincerity). The discovery of underlying brain states, like the discovery of underlying atomic structures, could provide a basis for establishing laws that relate those brain states to dispositions (in the case of people) like those that relate atomic structures to these dispositions (in the case of metals).

In the case of the atomic theory of matter, certain kinds of explanatory circularity were thereby eliminated. Instead of explaining why this thing is yellow by observing that it is *gold* and that things that are *gold* are yellow by definition, it would be appropriate to explain that it has a certain atomic structure— namely, atomic number 79—and that things of that kind have yellow among their permanent properties. Moreover, it would now be possible to explain why other things that might resemble *gold* in some ways (such as color and appearance) may not resemble *gold* in other ways due to differences in their atomic structure, as is the case with "fool's gold".

Surely, the atomic theory of matter assumes its significance because the atomic structure of things is lawfully related to their other properties (as dispositions toward behavior). And the study of neuroscience assumes its significance because the neurology of human brain states is likewise lawfully related to other human properties (as dispositions toward behavior). Indeed, if atomic numbers and brain states were *not* lawfully related to these other properties (as dispositions toward behavior), it is difficult to imagine why they would be of scientific interest. That is the reason why.

A nice illustration of this point can be derived from the speculation—an exercise of imagination to which philosophers, especially, are prone—that we (you and I) might be nothing more than merely *brains in vats*. A fascinating example can be found in the movie, *The Man With Two Brains*. The hero of this film (played by Steve Martin), it turns out, has the unusual ability to communicate telepathically with one specific brain in a vat, which happens to be the brain of a woman. He falls in love with her and, in the course of the plot's development, arranges for its substitution with that of his wife (played by Kathleen Turner), who is beautiful but a shrew.

No doubt, the fictional capacity to communicate telepathically was introduced to overcome the obvious problems that arise when someone has no mouth, throat, vocal chords, diaphragm or lungs. Indeed, if someone were nothing more than a brain in a vat, it is not easy to see not only how she could communicate (or interact) with anyone else but also how she could receive information (or stimulation) from the environment around her. It is easier to imagine that thought processes might occur as effects of shifts between brain states, but not how other of these phenomena could occur.

WHERE IN THE WORLD ARE MEANINGS?

The speculation that we might be nothing more than brains in vats is a recent development in a philosophical tradition professing skepticism about the knowledge we are capable of possessing about ourselves and the world around us. The position known as *solipsism*, for example, maintains that none of us can even prove that there is "a world around us". According to solipsism, it is impossible to demonstrate that (what we take to be) the external world is anything more than a construction of our mind. Indeed, strictly speaking, it is impossible for anyone to prove that anyone besides themselves exists. The only thing there is might be your mind!

Descartes went even further and was concerned with whether or not we could establish our own existence to ourselves. He was troubled by the possibility that his experience might result from illusions, delusions, and hallucinations. In order to be certain that he should not be deceived or misled by things he only imagined he knew or thought he experienced, Descartes introduced the conception of an *Evil Genius*, who would deceive him and mislead him in every case where that might be possible, such as inducing him to think he was sitting in his den (when he was dreaming) or tricking him into imagining he was alone (when he was hallucinating).

In Chapter 4, we shall consider how Descartes coped with this problem. What I want you to notice now is that the notion that we might be nothing but brains in vats belongs to a distinguished philosophical tradition. Moreover, it has proven nettlesome even for very distinguished philosophers. Hilary Putnam, for example, contends that the hypothesis that we may be brains in vats *cannot possibly be true*—that it is, in a certain sense, "self-refuting" (Putnam 1981). Explaining the sense in which this hypothesis is supposed to be "self-refuting" is not an easy task, but ultimately depends upon a theory of his according to which "meanings just aren't in the head".

To indicate the general lines of an approach of this kind, suppose, for example, that brains in vats sometimes think about apple trees. We know that *apple trees* themselves are not in our heads, but it may come as some surprise to discover that *thoughts* of apple trees—or, perhaps better, that the *meaning* of thoughts about apple trees—are not in our heads either! A possible explanation for this puzzling situation might be that the existence of "meanings" depends upon the existence of causal connections between whatever we think by means of and whatever we think about. Without causal connections between ideas and things, there might be no thoughts.

A causal theory of this kind would make meanings dependent upon causal connections between minds (or their contents) and things existing in the world. From this point of view, therefore, the hypothesis that we are nothing but brains in vats might appear to be "self-refuting" because those brains have thoughts with thought content that could not exist but for presumptive past occurrences of suitable causal interactions with things in the world! It may be for this reason that Putnam's discussion of brains in vats assumes that these brains were removed from our bodies by some mad scientist and placed into vats after having had experiences of this kind.

Putnam's arguments are ingenious, but they may or may not be persuasive. As we shall consider again in Chapter 4, there are various kinds of properties and entities for which causal theories of this kind—now usually called "causal theories of reference"—appear highly implausible. One such case is that of *non-existent entities*, such as werewolves and vampires, on the one hand, and Santa Claus and Mary Poppins, on the other. Surely we can think about things of those kinds and persons such as these without having to encounter them! If a causal approach of this kind were correct, it would be difficult to see how we could think about non-existent things.

Perhaps meanings *are* in the head, after all! Without attempting to settle this question now, especially since it is a matter to which we shall return, observe that the prospect that we might be brains in vats raises at least two kinds of problems. One is how content might get into those brains; the other is how behavior might get out. In *The Man With Two Brains*, the second problem was solved telepathically. In Putnam's version, the first problem was resolved by positing previous experience. It is not obvious, however, that either approach yields a suitable solution.

FROM FOLK PSYCHOLOGY TO COGNITIVE SCIENCE

The hypothesis that we might be brains in vats does not appear to be amenable to a purely conceptual refutation of the kind that Putnam advocates. Like its philosophical predecessors, it appears to describe a possibility that is *not* self-refuting and therefore requires a response. In order to cope with this problem, however, it is essential to beware of unstated assumptions. If the challenge is advanced to "demonstrate" or to "prove" that we are not brains in vats, we must not fall into the trap of assuming that our reasoning has to be *conclusive*. It may be that this is a problem that falls into the domain of inconclusive reasoning instead.

The most adequate framework for approaching this problem, which we will explore further in Chapter 3, is that of attempting to discover an explanation that would account for the observable phenomena more adequately than any of its alternatives. Technically, this kind of reasoning is known as "inference to the best explanation". The question thus becomes, in relation to solipsism, for example, is the hypothesis that the world is but a construction of my mind the most reasonable explanation for everything that I experience? Admittedly, it is a *possible* explanation. Is it *the best*?

A contrary argument might go like this. If the world were nothing but a construction of my mind, then why is it not a kinder and a gentler place? After all, if the world really were *nothing more* than a product of my own imagination, then why isn't it closer to my heart's desire? Why is it so full of threats and promises? of good and evil? of pain and disease? Perhaps even if it were a product of my own imagination, I could not exercise control over *everything* that happens. But how is it that I exercise control over so little of what happens? Why don't things turn out my way more often?

The argument demands that we take into account all the available evidence in the form of the totality of our experience. It does not provide us with a conclusive answer to the question. But it does suggest that, even if the world *might be* a construction of our mind, there are other hypotheses that appear far more reasonable. The hypothesis that we are limited and fallible members of the human community who, for the most part, have to work hard and compete with others for what we want appears to provide an alternative, which more adequately accounts for the world around us.

The hypothesis that we might be brains in vats, like solipsism before it, challenges us to reflect upon the kinds of evidence we have in relation to unusual conjectures. But similar reasoning applies even in everyday surroundings. If you were to ask yourself what day of the year it is and how you happen to know, you might be surprised. Many small evidential indicators influence your belief, ranging from radio announcements and television schedules to newspaper datelines and such. It is possible that these diverse sources are being manipulated to deceive you into forming the wrong belief. Ordinarily, however, that would be a silly thing to think.

Nevertheless, the hypothesis that we might be brains in vats help us to contemplate how much more there is to human beings even as thinking things than what is situated between our ears. In order for content to get into our heads, we need some means for its aquisition. And for behavior to get out, we need some means for its production. Both of these considerations suggest that there is more to human beings than brains and raise the possibility that *our bodies* may make an important difference to cognition. Perhaps the hypothesis that we might be brains in vats derives its ultimate importance from the realization that we must be so much more.

Consider a simple model of a possible cognitive system with a brain and a body. The properties of that system, presumably, would include:

(a) sense receptors for acquiring information from the environment;
(b) some means for internal information processing by the brain; and,
(c) motor activity activators relating system states to system behavior.

In the case of normal human beings, task (a) is accomplished by means of sense organs, such as those for sight, taste, hearing and smell; task (b) is accomplished by means of mental operations; task (c) is accomplished by nerve and muscle activators that produce verbal and other behavior.

The advent of the computing machine has brought in its wake a new approach toward understanding the nature of the mind, which is often referred to as "cognitive science". This movement has been inspired by the realization that the conditions that a cognitive system must fulfill as described above bear a striking similarity to those of computer systems, which acquire information from their environments as (a′) *input*, then process that information through the execution of (b′) *a program,* which produces behavior by a system in the form of (c′) *output*. From this perspective, human beings and computing machines appear strikingly alike.

Moreover, if the analogy between computing machines and thinking things can be sustained, then thought processes themselves might turn out to be mechanical and minds nothing more than special kinds of machines. A conception that applies to computing machines may turn out to also apply to human beings, namely, that they are both *special kinds* of causal systems, which shift from a state *S1* at a time *t1* to a state *S2* at a time *t2* in accordance with a program. We are going to explore this conception in the chapters that follow, so pay special attention to some of the key ideas involved here, such as "input", "output" and "program".

The computational conception is quite commonly described as a kind of *functionalism*, where functionalism envisions the purpose of computers to be the execution of functions. Functions, in turn, tend to be envisioned as algorithms, which are specific sequences of steps whose satisfaction is guaranteed to yield the solution to a problem (where problems of arithmetic serve as illustrations: given suitable input, yield your income for the year as output and calculate federal and state taxes due thereupon). Thus, the theory that minds are causal systems which execute functions in the form of programs is *machine state* functionalism (Putnam 1961).

In technical discourse and in daily life, certain terms are ambiguous. We have already discovered that "cognitive science" is one such phrase, sometimes standing for the domain of inquiry and other times standing for the computational research program. The term "functionalism" likewise has at least two meanings, since "causal role" functionalism must be distinguished from "machine state" functionalism. *Causal role* functionalism identifies the meaning of a concept with its causal role in influencing behavior without presuming that minds are computers, that thought is computation or that there are mental algorithms (Fetzer 1994).

During the course of this book, you will encounter what appear to be at least three distinct conceptions of cognition. According to the computational conception, cognition is *computation over representations*. That is "the classic conception" of minds as computers. When it comes to the connectionist conception, however, there are at least two alternative interpretations. One is that cognition is *computation across distributed representations*. This differs from the classic conception because minds are "a different kind" of computer using different kinds of representations.

The third and final is that cognition is a *causal process involving distributed representations*. On this conception, minds are not computers, even though they can function as if they were, and cognition is not computation. Although I suggest in Chapter 6 that the semiotic conception of mentality introduced in Chapter 5 fits the connectionist conception of the brain "like hand and glove", I want to emphasize here that this relationship depends upon adopting the third of these concepts of cognition. It completes a transition from machine state to causal role functionalism that we are going to explore.

CHAPTER THREE

MINDS AND MACHINES

TURING MACHINES

Laws of nature differ from laws of society, with which you are probably far more familiar. For one thing, laws of society are created, but laws of nature are discovered. For another, laws of society can be changed, but laws of nature are unchangeable. For a third, laws of society must be enforced, but laws of nature cannot be violated. Speed limits on highways, legal drinking ages in bars, and requirements for citizens to vote are relevant examples of laws of society that must be created, could be changed, and can be violated.

If you read Chapters 1 and 2 carefully, you will have noticed that lawlike sentences are defined and universal generalizations are defined, but the exact relationship between them is not made explicit. That turns out to be an important question, because a universal generalization might be true simply as a matter of accident (say, when every Ferrari just happens to be painted red) rather than because the attribute actually is a permanent property of a reference property. A universal generalization will be a lawlike sentence *only if* there are no physical processes that could separate those properties.

Consequently, every lawlike sentence is a universal generalization, but not every universal generalization is a lawlike sentence. Since lawlike sentences assert the *nonexistence* of even a single physical process that could separate an instance of its attribute from an instance of its reference property, they have the force of what are known as *negative existential* sentences. Even if every Ferrari were painted red (say, as a co-incidence or as a factory policy), that relationship cannot be both lawlike and true, because there is at least one physical process (repainting) that could change it.

When the question of machine mentality arises within cognitive science, it is important to understand the kind of issue being raised. Almost no one today believes that contemporary machines—the computers that are available now—have the capacity to think. The question being raised instead is whether inanimate machines could ever be constructed that would possess at least some of the mental powers of human beings. The answer to such a question is affirmative only if that possibility does not violate natural laws.

Suppose we were to agree that every inanimate machine that the world *has ever seen* has lacked the mental powers of human beings. Would that mean that every inanimate machine the world *will ever see* must also lack the mental powers of human beings? If you understand the distinctions I have already drawn, you know the answer to this question should be "No!" And the explanation you could give to justify your reply is that this may be merely a universal generalization that is true by accident rather than a law.

One of the reasons it is plausible to believe that a machine might have a mind is that many important innovations promoting progress in cognitive science have arisen from developments in computer technology. The development of machines with the capacity to solve problems that previously required the application of mentality has suggested the possibility that these machines and human beings may be fundamentally the same in certain crucial respects—not concerning their physical origins, which are quite different, but regarding their mode of operation, which conceivably could be the same.

Another reason it is plausible to believe that someday a machine might have a mind is the close connection that may obtain between computability and thought. Indeed, there are those who contend that the theory of computability defines the boundaries of thought, precisely because all thought is computational. This idea is rather deep and will demand our concentration. At least one philosopher has been sufficiently captivated by this notion that he has proposed, "Why not suppose that people *just are* computers and send philosophy packing?" (Haugeland, 1981, p. 5), which is a very good question.

In order to appreciate why this prospect is so enticing, it is necessary to understand the nature of computers and of computability. Our purpose here is not to become experts in the theory of computability (which is a challenging domain) but to become familiar with the general features of this terrain. The place to begin, I believe, is with the idea of the special kind of machine known as a Universal Turing Machine (Turing, 1950). This conception originated with Alan Turing (1912–1954), who was a brilliant British mathematician and logician.

The basic notion of a Turing Machine is fairly simple. It is a device that consists of a mechanism for making a mark on a roll of tape, which functions as a memory for the system. The mechanism can perform just four types of operations: It can make a mark; it can remove a mark; it can move the tape forward; and it can move the tape backward. The tape itself is divided into segments (or "cells"), each of which may or may not be marked, and must be of unlimited length. No matter how much tape we use, there is always more.

When the machine is provided with a "program" that instructs it what to do (when to mark and when to unmark, etc.), then it formally qualifies as a Turing Machine. Any marks with which it begins can be viewed as "input" and any marks that remain when its program has been executed can be viewed as "output." Were two marks on adjacent cells, for example, a specific program might cause the machine to mark three more cells to produce five marks together (perhaps thereby adding two and three to obtain five).

The distinction between "special purpose" and "general

purpose" machines arises here. Turing Machines that are designed to operate on the basis of just one set of instructions are "special purpose" machines. Universal Turing Machines, however, can imitate the performance of any special purpose machine when provided with the corresponding program. Because they can process any program that any Turing Machine can process, Universal Turing Machines are "general purpose" rather than only "special purpose" machines.

The striking feature of a Universal Turing Machine is that, although not complicated in design, it happens to possess enormous computational power. Alonzo Church, the great formal logician, has proven that a Universal Turing Machine is powerful enough to imitate any formal system, where a "formal system" consists of any collection of arbitrary elements and rules for their manipulation (so long as operations on the elements depend exclusively on their formal properties). Formal systems with which you are already familiar include every branch of mathematics, including arithmetic, algebra, and so forth.

The difference between a modern digital computer and a Universal Turing Machine is a matter of design rather than of power. Although they can employ a richer set of basic operations, as Philip Johnson-Laird (1988) has observed, anything that can be computed by these newer digital machines can also be computed by Universal Turing Machines. There is a fundamental sense in which Universal Turing Machines thereby exhaust the boundaries of the computable, since problems they cannot solve are not computable problems.

What contemporary philosophers, such as John Haugeland, have found so rich and exciting about these results is that they raise the possibility that the mind might be a computational device like a Universal Turing Machine. For, if this were the case, then the theory of computability *would* define the boundaries of thought, because all thought *would* be computational. Indeed, this vision has generated enormous enthusiasm throughout the cognitive science community, since it provides a unified conception of the nature of mind.

THE IMITATION GAME

No one would want to deny that the computational conception of mentality provides an immensely appealing framework for understanding both human beings and digital machines. The question is not whether it is attractive, but whether it is true. And this question turns out to be extremely difficult to answer. Indeed, much of the rest of this book is devoted to discovering a tentative answer to this question. Notice, in particular, that if it is true, then every computational contraption, whether human being or digital machine, is endowed with a mind, provided it is a formal system of this special kind.

One of the most appealing features of this conception is that it promises to resolve problems about which very little is known (the nature of the human mind) with answers about which a great deal is known (the theory of computing machines). Since no one doubts that current digital computers are computing machines (as special kinds of "automated" formal systems), the crucial question becomes whether or not human minds are also formal systems of this special kind. Unless human beings operate in the same fashion as digital machines, the computational conception cannot be sustained.

If human beings are automated formal systems, how can we tell? As it happens, Turing himself suggested an indirect approach toward the answer to this question. The problem that he wanted to address directly is that of whether inanimate machines can think, but his solution holds promise for our question, too. You might find this approach intriguing, because Turing proposed that at least some of the similarities and differences between human beings and digital machines could be measured by means of a game.

The game that Turing introduced is called the "Imitation

Game." It consists of three participants, a man, a woman, and an interrogator, who may be of either sex. The interrogator remains in a space separated from the other two and communicates with them by means of some device, such as a teletype machine, that will not give the game away. The objective of the game is for the interrogator to determine who is the man and who is not. The constraints imposed by the rules make it necessary for the interrogator to arrive at his guess solely on the basis of answers given to his questions.

The man is permitted to distort the truth, but the woman is required to answer truthfully. She might respond to a question by insisting, "I am the woman; don't listen to him!", but that would be to no avail, since the man could do the same. All by itself, the Imitation Game amounts to little more than another way to pass the time in a social setting. But Turing realized that any other property might do just as well as trying to guess someone's sex, and, indeed, for some purposes other questions would do even better.

Consider, for example, substituting an inanimate machine for the man. The question might then be changed to guessing which is the machine and which the human being. This is a much more intriguing proposition, since it suggests that behavioral criteria might support the inference that something is a thinking thing. If an interrogator could not distinguish between the human being and the inanimate machine on the basis of their answers to the questions that he might pose, then it would seem reasonable to infer that both parties were equal in relation to the property in question.

The underlying criterion that would apply here would be the capability of an inanimate machine to deceive a human being into thinking that it was human, too. But this approach can be pursued in yet another direction, since any test that pits an inanimate machine against a human being likewise pits a human being against an inanimate machine. The Imitation Game, after all, could also be employed to assess whether the responses of both participants were sufficiently similar to infer that they were produced by similar modes of operation. The evidence might suggest that they are both computational.

This sounds very plausible until we ask ourselves exactly what conclusions the results of the Imitation Game could be expected to sustain. Return to the first version, for example, consisting of a man, a woman, and an interrogator. The question here was a matter of sex: Which participant really is the man and which really is the woman? If the interrogator were misled into guessing incorrectly that the man was a woman or the woman was a man, what would that result have established? That the interrogator was misled, no doubt, but surely not that anyone there had actually changed their sex!

Return to the second version, consisting of an inanimate machine, a human being, and an interrogator once again. The question here was a matter of intellect: Which participant really is a thinking thing and which is merely an inanimate machine? If the interrogator were misled into guessing incorrectly that the inanimate machine was a thinking thing and that the human being was an inanimate machine, what would that result have established? It would not show that this human being actually is an inanimate machine. Would it be enough to show that an inanimate machine is a thinking thing?

Return to the third version, consisting of an inanimate machine, a human being, and an interrogator one more time. The question here is a matter of cognition: Are the participants' responses sufficiently similar to infer that they were produced by similar modes of operation? If they seemed to be quite similar, or perhaps even exactly the same, would that suggest that they are both computational systems? Could this test or any other like it provide a suitable foundation for arriving at the answer to this question?

THE CHINESE ROOM

It is an old saying that "if it looks like a duck, waddles like a duck, and quacks like a duck, then it's a duck!" But surely there are things of one kind that look and act (and even quack) like things of another kind without actually being them. This is something that hunters and actors have known for a long time. Is it something that we should suddenly forget? There is, after all, a fundamental distinction to be drawn between looking like, acting like, and quacking like the real thing as opposed to in fact being one. Con artists and frauds, alas, benefit from our gullibility on this point every single day.

These reflections strongly suggest that some additional distinctions are required if we want to understand how the Imitation Game leads us astray. If we borrow the term "function" from mathematics, where a function maps the elements of a domain onto a range (just as the function $x + 4 = y$ maps the value of $x + 4$ on the left onto the value of y, for any specific value of x), then the modes of operation of human beings and digital machines can be compared.

	DIGITAL MACHINES	HUMAN BEINGS
DOMAIN	Input	Stimuli
FUNCTION	Program	Process
RANGE	Output	Response

Figure 1. The Basic Analogy

It appears plausible, for example, to view programs as functions from inputs to outputs and to envision processes as functions from stimuli to responses.

There are at least three points of view that we could adopt

with respect to this comparison. Notice, in particular, that there are decided similarities between the input of a digital machine in relation to its output and the stimuli of a human being in relation to his responses. Precisely how far this can be carried is a matter we shall consider as we proceed. For the time being, you should observe that, especially in relation to the Imitation Game itself, *questions* could certainly serve as "input" for a machine or as "stimuli" for a human and *answers* could certainly serve as "output" and as "responses."

Even if different systems provide the same answers to the same questions, however, that would not mean that they arrive at those answers by the same modes of operation. Sometimes we understand what we are talking about, sometimes we merely memorize what we want to say, and sometime we simply read words off a screen (remember Ronald Reagan?). That the same input/stimulus is invariably or probably associated with the same output/response is not sufficient evidence to infer what causes these effects.

The first distinction that needs to be drawn, therefore, is between types of systems that yield the same output/responses when subject to the same input/stimuli but that produce them by means of *different* programs/processes and those that yield the same output/responses when subject to the same input/ stimuli and actually produce them by means of the *same* programs/processes. In cases of the first kind, relations of simulation obtain between them. In cases of the second kind, relations of replication obtain.

Once the difference between simulation and replication has been recognized, it is not difficult to realize that the Imitation Game affords a suitable evidential foundation for drawing inferences about the degree to which two systems stand in relations of *simulation*, but that it does not afford a suitable evidential foundation for drawing inferences about the degree to which two systems stand in relations of *replication*. This should come as no surprise, I suppose, since the rules of the game restrict the evidence to questions and answers that are publicly observable. Yet this difference is easy to ignore.

The distinction between simulation and replication has been implicitly emphasized by the American philosopher John Searle in an argument that is known as the Chinese Room. Searle's argument is presented in the form of a "thought experiment" (Searle, 1984). A thought experiment differs from an ordinary experiment because you merely think things through from a certain point of view rather than conduct observations and measurements or otherwise causally interact with the world. (The benefits of "thinking things through," no doubt, can be quite important, a point to which we are going to return.)

Imagine that someone (Searle himself, for example) is locked into an enclosed room with one entry through which Chinese symbols are sometimes sent in and one exit through which Chinese symbols can be sent out. Then, if the occupant of that room were fluent in English but ignorant of Chinese, yet had access to a book of instructions, written in English, directing him to send certain symbols out when certain other symbols were sent in, it might appear to outside observers as if he understood Chinese, when he does not.

Notice how cleverly this thought experiment satisfies the constraints imposed by simulation situations and does not satisfy the conditions required by replication situations. Indeed, Searle himself suggests that the symbols coming in might be called "input," the symbols going out "output," and the book of instructions a "program." Yet, even though the observable behavior of this input-output program might resemble the observable behavior of a real scholar of Chinese, those systems would only simulate but not replicate each other.

When we look back upon the Imitation Game itself, from this point of view, it is striking to realize that, even in the first instance, if a male were to answer questions that led to the interrogator to guess (mistakenly) that he is female, this result would have been caused by a successful simulation. Analogously, in the second instance, were an inanimate machine to answer questions that led the interrogator to guess (mistakenly) that it is a human being, this result, too, would have been the effect of a successful simulation.

The third instance raises at least one difficulty we have not addressed before, even when we approach it from this point of view. We have taken for granted that digital machines can imitate formal systems, which poses no problems on its own. But suppose we acknowledge that human beings can imitate formal systems, too. After all, every branch of mathematics *is* a formal system, and human beings *can* add and subtract. Does that mean inanimate machines possess some of the mental powers of human beings?

There is more than one possible answer to this question, depending on what we mean by the words we have used. If by "imitation" we mean the same thing we mean by "simulation," the answer appears to be "Yes!" But if by "imitation" we mean the same thing we mean by "replication," the answer might instead be "No!" Human beings and digital machines both have the capacity to *simulate* formal systems, but that does not decide the issue of whether they simulate formal systems by *the same* modes of operation!

The problem is subtle, and the issues at stake are easily misunderstood. This perplexing situation has even led a well-known American philosopher, Fred Dretske, to deny that inanimate machines can even add and subtract! On initial consideration, after all, this sounds like a very peculiar claim, especially since we use pocket calculators to add and subtract all the time. On further reflection, it should be apparent that what he is really after is that there may be an important difference in how these things do what they do.

UNDERSTANDING NATURAL LANGUAGE

The distinction between simulation and replication strongly suggests that the Imitation Game cannot succeed when it is employed to ascertain whether or not inanimate machines are thinking things. In this form, it is often known as the "Turing Test." Is there nothing then that can be said on its behalf? In fact, at least two lines of reasoning could be advanced in an effort to salvage the significance of the Turing Test, one of which has little to recommend it, but the other of which poses a very important challenge.

The first defense attempts to capitalize on the language that was used in describing the Turing Test itself. The underlying criterion, you may recall, was the capability of an inanimate machine to deceive a human being into thinking that it was human, too. But surely, it could be claimed, something has the capacity "to deceive" or "to attempt to deceive" another thing only if it has motives and beliefs, which is already enough to establish that the inanimate machine really is a thinking thing in spite of our distinctions.

This line of reasoning, I am afraid, sounds better than it should. Were the interrogator to mistakenly conclude about an inanimate machine that it is a human being, the only motives and beliefs that would thereby have been displayed are those of the interrogator, not those of the machine. The behavior of the machine, with respect to its inputs and outputs, was indeed the evidence by means of which the interrogator arrived at his conclusion. It is only a manner of speaking to say that the machine deceived the man.

As a result, the first defense really doesn't have a great deal to recommend it. The language that we use to describe situations such as these can be a valuable resource in exploring issues of this kind, but it can sometimes be misleading. What is most important to understand about this line of reasoning is that, by endorsing the description that machines have the capacity to deceive human beings, it takes for granted the answer to the question we want to answer. Anyone who argues this way therefore "begs the question."

In order for this argument to succeed, it would have to be the case that we can be more confident when a machine deceives a human being than we can that a machine is a thinking thing. *If* a machine could deceive a human being, *then* it would be a thinking thing. But to justify the claim that the antecedent of this conditional (the "if" sentence) is true, it would have to be established as the conclusion of an independent argument. Otherwise, the consequent of this conditional (the "then" sentence) might or might not be true.

Begging the question is a popular practice among philosophers, because it makes it easier—often *much* easier—to establish their conclusions. If the second line of reasoning in defense of the Turing Test commits this fallacy, it does so in a far more subtle fashion. This defense has been advanced by William J. Rapaport, a philosopher and computer scientist, who thinks that the Turing Test might survive the damage it suffered in the Chinese Room. His position emphasizes the importance of understanding natural language (Rapaport, 1988).

A natural language is one that has been spoken by some population of human beings in the world. The most familiar example for readers of this book, no doubt, is English. But French, German, Russian, and the like are all on a par as illustrations. In Rapaport's view, since the Turing Test hinges on the capacity to answer questions expressed in natural language, the criterion that it employs to identify thinking things is the capacity to understand natural language. The things that can understand natural language, he suggests, are the same things that properly qualify as thinking things.

There are several reasons why this proposal is an important one. The idea that there is an intimate connection between language and thought is even more plausible than the idea that there is an intimate connection between thought and computability. If language turns out to be a computational phenomenon, of course, they might both be true—an issue we shall pursue in Chapter 4. Even more importantly, understanding natural language appears to be far more central to what it takes to have a mind than whether or not an inanimate machine could possibly fool a human being.

THE PROBLEM OF OTHER MINDS

There are three great problems in the philosophy of mind: first, the nature of mind; second, the relation of mind to body; and, third, the existence of other minds. The first problem is crucial to the other two, since it would be impossible to ascertain the relation of mind to body or the existence of other minds without knowing the nature of mind. Indeed, one of the early lessons of a scientific education is to understand the hypothesis that you want to investigate *before* undertaking its investigation. We are in the position of pursuing the third question without answering the first.

But we have made some progress. We have assumed that human beings are thinking things, but we do not yet know what makes this so. We have accepted the possibility that inanimate machines might be thinking things, but we don't know how to tell. We have discovered the distinction between simulation and replication, which has proven to be quite helpful. We have divorced the physical features of specific systems from their cognitive capabilities. And we have separated the behavior displayed by the answering of questions from the state of understanding natural language.

Even if an inanimate machine could fool a human being, it is not very likely that you would be tempted to think that this ability is what it takes to be a thinking thing. After all, there are those (perhaps not many) who never deceive anyone at all, yet that does not compromise their standing as thinking things. This capacity appears to be more like a symptom, such as good grades and high SAT scores, that functions as a usually reliable evidential indicator of the presence of a certain trait, such as high intelligence.

The presence of symptoms can be helpful as evidence that ought to be considered, but they may not be available and are not actually required. A person can have high intelligence even though he had terrible grades and did poorly on his SATs. (You may have already observed this yourself.) A youngster raised in a difficult family environment, with parents at each other's throat, might be too emotionally distracted to do well in school. If the house caught fire and you had no sleep the night before, it would not be especially surprising to find that this did not improve your SAT scores.

We already know that cognitive attributes are "theoretical," because their presence or absence cannot be determined simply by public inspection. These considerations suggest that these attributes are "conditional" as well, because their effects are only displayed under appropriate test conditions. The presence or absence of properties that are both theoretical and conditional poses difficult problems for scientific inquiries, since the only mode of access to them is by "inference to the best explanation."

Inference to the best explanation involves selecting the hypothesis that, if true, would provide the best explanation for the relevant available evidence. It can be viewed as a process of trial and error, of conjectures and refutations, or of successive approximation, as one hypothesis after another is investigated and discarded. Sometimes the only explanation that can account for all the evidence seems implausible considered on its own. As Sherlock Holmes once noted, "After you have eliminated the impossible, whatever is left, however improbable, must be the truth."

An explanation that qualifies as "the best explanation" within a scientific inquiry must be conditional, testable, and tentative, as we learned in Chapter 1. The problems that we now confront, which range from the Imitation Game to the Turing Test to the Chinese Room, therefore, challenge us to discover "the best explanation" for behavior of different kinds—from answering questions by means of a teletype machine to transmitting Chinese symbols to understanding natural languages. Are any of these cases that have to be explained by positing the existence of minds?

The most demanding condition imposed by a reliance upon inference to the best explanation is exposing the full range of alternatives that are available. In the case of the problem of other minds, it can be helpful to begin with the classical version directed at the existence of other *human* minds. In this version, in other words, the question becomes: How can I know whether or not there are any *other* humans with minds like mine? Does anyone else have a mind? Or could everyone else be without one?

Some of the most fascinating examples of alternative explanations of behavior that simulates human behavior without necessarily involving human minds are found at the movies. In *The Stepford Wives*, for example, the men replace their wives with physically identical but mentally vacuous counterparts. *Alien* features a science officer who turns out to be a completely lifelike but synthetic robot. *The Terminator* stars the exterior of a human with the interior of a Cyberdyne Systems Model 101.

What is fascinating about these films, I believe, is that they are constructed around scenarios that might or might not be physically possible. Which are possible and which are not, we do not yet know. Nothing about their settings suggests that they are absurd or merely works of fantasy. They appear to be consistent with the principles of logic, compatible with the history of the world up until now, and not precluded by natural laws. They are plausible extensions of the history of the world in which we now reside.

A second version of the problem of other minds is directed toward the existence of other *animals* with minds. All too often this alternative has been presented (in the media, at least) as merely reflecting the possibility that other animals might have *human* minds. The case of Mr. Ed, the talking horse, comes immediately to mind, but the entire series of *Planet of the Apes* movies provides a vivid illustration. On rare occasion, the possibility of other animals with nonhuman minds receives some consideration. "Flipper" is an instance. But it is the rare exception.

The third version of the problem of other minds, of course, is devoted to the prospect that *machines* might have minds. The machines that matter here tend to be Universal Turing Machines, current digital machines, and connectionist machines (which we shall consider in Chapter 6). Researchers in this domain have been preoccupied with *human* mentality and with *human* cognition, precisely because human mentality and human cognition are what they want to capture. That is their objective.

There are trivial and nontrivial versions of such questions concerning the existence of other minds. Since human beings are animals, too, it is not difficult to establish that at least some animals have minds (human minds, at that). The most trivial case, therefore, would hold that, at least, *I* am an animal and *I* have a mind (which you can repeat on your own behalf). When "machines" are defined as systems that can perform work, it is easy to show that at least some machines (us) also have (human) minds.

But the nontrivial versions of these questions are another matter altogether. Indeed, in advancing these "solutions" to the trivial versions of these questions, I could be accused of having committed the philosopher's fallacy of begging the question myself. I have assumed something that I surely ought to be proving instead, namely, that *I* have a mind! After all, what is it about me that justifies that inference?

If I cannot establish that *I* have a mind, how could I possibly conclude that some animals and some machines have minds? You should appreciate this quandary, because you are in it, too! In the chapters that follow, therefore, we shall try to solve it.

CHAPTER FOUR

THE NATURE OF LANGUAGE

PHYSICAL SYMBOL SYSTEMS

It may seem odd to mention movies in an introduction to cognitive science. But, from a scientific point of view, what matters is how well an idea stands up to experience rather than where it came from. The scenarios of motion pictures are an interesting source of ideas for several reasons, one of which is that they are familiar to younger readers today. There was a time when allusions to works of English literature—by Chaucer, Milton, or Shakespeare, for example—were the bread and butter of conversational language. Those times, alas, are long past, and television and the movies are upon us.

More strikingly, the capacity of the entertainment industry to consume ideas is almost limitless. New ideas command a premium, especially those with the potential to entertain millions on television and at the cinema. To meet that nearly insatiable demand requires the creative talents of numerous authors and editors, who collectively constitute an enormous resource with respect to exercising their capacity for imagination and conjecture. It would certainly be a mistake to ignore such a promising avalanche of ideas.

A distinction is often drawn between the "context of discovery" and the "context of justification." The context of discovery concerns the source of an idea, while the context of justification concerns how well such an idea is able to withstand critical scrutiny. Works of fiction, including films, are entirely acceptable as sources of ideas (within the context of discovery), but they are inappropriate as warrants for their truth (within the context of justification). When the truth of those ideas is at stake, there is no substitute for evidence.

Exactly what counts as evidence within the domain of cognitive science has not always been entirely clear. Descartes, for example, believed that he could provide a demonstration of his existence as a thinking thing by means of the argument *"Cogito, ergo sum!"* ("I think, therefore I am!") One reason that Descartes felt so confident about this argument was that the more that he doubted, questioned, or challenged it, the more convinced he became of his own existence as a doubting, questioning, or challenging (thinking) thing.

Some scholars have wondered why Descartes did not adopt some other version of this argument, such as, say, *"Sudeo, ergo sum!"* ("I perspire, therefore I am!") And, indeed, this is another very good question, because if the premise "I perspire" could be established on suitable grounds, the conclusion "I am!" would follow no less validly than it would follow from the original. Descartes preferred "I think" to "I perspire" ("I eat," "I sleep," and all the rest) because only this one among them offers the prospect of certainty.

The difference is degree of conviction. Descartes knew of the possibility of illusions, delusions, and hallucinations. He felt that he could be deceived about his existence as *any* kind of thing—even as a perspiring thing—except as a doubting, questioning, and challenging (thinking) thing. And he drew the conclusion that what he was—what he really was—was a thinking thing: *"Sum res cogitans!"* ("I am a thing that thinks!"). Were this view to be generalized across the human species, it would imply that what it is to be a human—the nature of human nature—is to be an instance of the kind which thinks.

The most troublesome element of Descartes' position from the perspective of the philosophy of science today, I suspect, is its emphasis on certainty as the foundation of knowledge. "Certainty," in the Cartesian sense, is a function of *indubita-*

bility, of the incapacity to be subject to doubt. Of course, there are things that we find impossible (or almost impossible) to doubt, including (for most of us) that we exist, that we had parents, and that they had parents before them. We assume that our parents were human, that our parents' parents were human, etc., as though that sequence could go on forever.

You do not have to be an evolutionary theoretician to realize that, insofar as human beings ascended from other species, it is physically impossible for every human being to have had human beings as parents (note the regress)! The reason that this is interesting here, moreover, is that, apart from this reflection, we probably would have had no reason to doubt that the parents of a human being must be human beings themselves. We have discovered that this "indubitable" hypothesis is not just doubtful, but almost certainly false.

This result may show that indubitability is not an infallible guide to the truth. It does not show that Descartes' conception of human beings as thinking things is false. The problem that arises with the Cartesian account is to express the idea of what it is to be a thinking thing sufficiently clearly that it can be the subject of empirical inquiry. Otherwise, the *cogito* reflects cognition without science, rather than a science of cognition. It occurs as an object of philosophical speculation rather than a topic of scientific investigation.

A solution to this problem might occur if thinking things could be understood as machines of a certain special kind. Such an approach has been proposed by Alan Newell and Herbert Simon (1976), two influential computer scientists at Carnegie-Mellon University. They suggest that thinking things (they talk about "intelligent" things, but the difference does not matter here) are best viewed as *physical symbol systems*, as special kinds of Turing Machines (or automated formal systems), which can manipulate symbols.

Within the context of Newell and Simon's theory, *symbols* are physical patterns that can occur as elements of another type of entity that they call an expression (or a "symbol structure"). A *symbol structure*, in turn, is composed of a number of instances of symbols that are related in some physical way, such as one symbol being next to another. Newell and Simon's symbols are like the letters of the alphabet of an ordinary language, such as English, while expressions are more like the words and sentences we make of them.

A more descriptive name for systems of this kind might be to call them "expression-processing" (or "string-manipulating") systems. Symbol systems in Newell and Simon's sense are therefore similar to the automated formal systems we encountered in Chapter 3. Since both of these notions depend upon that of a Universal Turing Machine, what we really have are three different ways to refer to the behavior of systems of essentially the very same kind. Whether we call them "physical symbol systems," "automated formal systems," or "Universal Turing Machines" makes little difference in the end.

What is important about Newell and Simon's position is less a matter of the details of their conception of physical symbol systems than it is of the theory that it enables them to advance. For Newell and Simon contend that physical symbol systems possess the necessary and sufficient conditions for being intelligent. If this is true, then everything that is intelligent is a physical symbol system, and everything that is a physical symbol system is intelligent. If this is true, then if you and I (not to mention our dogs and cats) are intelligent, then the reason is that we (they) are things of this kind.

Newell and Simon's approach, no doubt, can be compared with Descartes'. Although Newell and Simon focus on "intelligence" and Descartes focuses on "thought," both are intended to capture what thinking is about. When viewed from this perspective, moreover, Newell and Simon's theory seems to be more encompassing than Descartes'. Part of its appeal is the promise that it might apply to inanimate machines as well as to human beings. It offers the prospect that inanimate machines as well as human beings might turn out to be thinking things, an outcome of which Descartes would not have approved.

Another potential advantage of the symbol system theory by comparison with the Cartesian conception is a matter of methodology. The only possible test of Descartes' account appears to be by way of the *cogito*. If Newell and Simon's account could be tested by other than deductive reasoning—such as by building some machines—it might be possible to adopt the methods that distinguish empirical inquiries (such as observation and experimentation) in the pursuit of thinking things. If the methods of empirical science could be utilized in the study of cognition, the result could be a science of cognition.

THE COMPUTATIONAL CONCEPTION

Several strands of thought come together at this juncture. One strand is the idea that thought requires language. If thought requires language and if language is a system of symbols, then thought requires a system of symbols. A second strand is the idea that thinking may involve nothing more than the manipulation of systems of symbols. If thinking involves nothing more than the manipulation of systems of symbols, then things that can manipulate symbols are thinking things. (The crucial issues revolve about these strands.)

Yet a third strand is the idea that symbol systems have the capacity for thought. If symbol systems are things that can manipulate systems of symbols and if the capacity for thought is nothing more than the ability to manipulate symbols, then symbol systems have the capacity for thought. A last strand is the idea that the existence of a thinking thing might be subjected to direct test. If the capacity for thought is nothing more than the ability to manipulate symbols, then tests that test the ability to manipulate symbols are tests that test the capacity for thought (the existence of thinking things).

Since all thought is computational if this conception is sound, it has come to be known as *the computational conception* of language and of mentality. This conception ties together the ideas of a Turing Machine, of an automated formal system, and of a physical symbol system with the notion that understanding natural language involves the ability to manipulate systems of symbols and that the Turing Test can provide a test of the existence of thinking things. They come together as a very tight and very attractive package deal.

Before turning to an evaluation of this conception, notice, especially, that the term "symbol system" occurs here in two different senses. One is that of a symbol system as *a system of symbols*, where "symbols" are physical patterns that can occur as elements of symbol structures when they are related in some physical way. The other is that of a symbol system as *a system that has the capacity to manipulate a system of symbols* in the sense that has already been defined. In the first sense, "symbol systems" are like languages, while, in the second sense, "symbol systems" are like the users of a language.

Exactly how much "symbol systems" in the first sense are like languages and exactly how much "symbol systems" in the second sense are like the users of a language turn out to be two extremely important questions. Things can be alike in some respects without being alike in all. Apples and oranges are both round and edible, but that does not make them the same in every respect. Systems of symbols and symbol systems could be similar to languages and language users, respectively, without being the very same things.

Because the computational conception supports the Turing Test as a test of mentality (or of "thinking things"), the results of Chapter 3 ought to make us suspect that the argument it presents might possibly be unsound. For, if the Turing Test is able to measure the extent to which two systems simulate one another's input/output behavior but is unable to measure the extent to which they replicate one another's internal modes of operation, perhaps the computational conception falls prey to the difference that is involved here.

Suppose we review the four strands that constitute the computational conception from this point of view. Notice, in particular, that it consists of a sequence of conditional ("if . . . then —") sentences, where the consequent of the first becomes the antecedent of the next. It therefore has the logical structure of four conditional sentences: "if A then B," "if B then C," "if C then D," and "if D then E." If this is an adequate analysis of its structure, then the position that it represents appears to be valid. But are these premises true?

Let's work backward from the fourth strand to the first. The last strand suggests that tests that test the ability to manipulate symbols are tests that test the capacity for thought, *provided* that the capacity for thought is nothing more than the ability to manipulate symbols. The Turing Test seems to be perfectly adequate as a test that tests the ability to manipulate symbols, but it does not appear to be adequate as a test of the capacity for thought. Possibly there is more to thought than the capacity to manipulate symbols.

The third strand maintains that symbol systems have the capacity for thought, *provided* that symbol systems are things that can manipulate symbols *and* that there is nothing more to thought than the capacity to manipulate symbols. The condition that symbol systems are things that can manipulate symbols, however, appears to be difficult to dispute, since this claim is true as a matter of definition. Its truth follows from the language of Newell and Simon's theory. If something is wrong here, then it must lie elsewhere.

The second strand asserts that things that can manipulate symbols are thinking things, *provided* that thinking involves nothing more than the manipulation of symbols. The consequent of this conditional appears to be true if its antecedent is true. But is it reasonable to suppose that thinking involves nothing more than the manipulation of symbols? A Turing

Machine has the capacity to perform exactly four kinds of operations. But is it reasonable to suppose that a Turing Machine (including its program) is a thinking thing?

The first strand, finally, contends that thought requires language, *provided* that thought requires language *and* language is a system of symbols. At least two issues arise here. One is whether the thesis that thought requires language ought to be interpreted to encompass *all* thought or merely *some*. If thinking ever takes place in images, for example, the "all" interpretation, which is significant, must be false. If thinking ever takes place in language, however, then the "some" interpretation must be true, but it is also trivial.

The other is whether language is a system of symbols in the sense that Newell and Simon intend. According to their conception, symbols are physical patterns that can occur as elements of symbol structures, which are created when a number of instances of symbols are related in "a physical way." The ways in which symbols can be related are functions of their shape, size, and location (such as when one symbol is next to another). These properties are known as "formal" properties of physical things, which is the underlying reason why symbol systems are also instances of automated formal systems.

THE PROBLEM OF REPRESENTATION

If there is more to thinking than the ability to manipulate symbols, or if there is more to language than its formal properties, there will be grounds to question the adequacy of the computational conception. The most important reason to doubt that it is adequate appears to be its failure to acknowledge that the words and sentences of English typically *stand for* (or "represent") objects and properties in the world. If we think of a language as consisting of a vocabulary and a grammar (the vocabulary and the grammar of English, say), this account seems to emphasize grammar at the expense of vocabulary.

That this is the case should come as no surprise when you consider that every operation that a symbol system can perform depends exclusively upon the formal properties of the symbols that it manipulates. Any property that does not qualify as a formal property is a property that purely computational devices—such as Turing Machines, automated formal systems, and symbol systems alike—cannot accommodate. These nonformal properties, including relations of representation to the world's objects and properties, are left out.

A few examples of formal symbols may help to make this consequence clear in relation to the English language. The alphabet of English includes twenty-six letters (from "a" to "z") and, when the natural numbers are included, an endless supply of numerals ("0," "1," "2," etc.). An arbitrary sequence of letters from this alphabet (say, "xyz") or of numerals from this set ("123") may not stand for anything. It would still be possible for these symbols to be manipulated by a machine, but that does not mean they represent anything at all.

You might object that the only reason these sequences do not stand for anything at all is because they were chosen at random. Other sequences of letters ("bat," "cat," "fat," etc.), after all, consist of elements from the English alphabet that do represent objects and properties of things in the world. If this approach were employed as a defense of the computational conception, however, by insisting that the only symbols that are subject to manipulation by symbol systems must stand for something in the world, it would thereby have demonstrated that the computational conception leaves something out.

The only alternative to this self-defeating defense thus appears to be to maintain that, in the case of human beings, at least, there is a built-in correspondence between the symbols that humans manipulate and what they are meant to represent. This position has been advanced by Fodor (1975), who contends that there is an innate *language of thought* (he calls it "mentalese") whose symbols stand for objects and properties in the world as a function of the structure of the human mind.

The only problem that we confront as we mature is to discover a correspondence between English, say, and mentalese.

Fodor's position here is reminiscent of the theory of knowledge as recollection, which was proposed by Plato (c. 427– c. 347 B.C.), one of the most influential of all philosophers. Plato conjectured that there is an "Eternal Mind," which is the repository of all knowledge, and that mortal minds participate in the Eternal Mind before birth. As a result, all knowledge resides in every mortal mind. We don't notice this, however, because the trauma of our birth causes us to forget everything we know, which is sometimes brought back to mind by events that occur during our lifetime, which trigger off recollections.

Fodor posits an innate universal language of thought that is possessed by every neurologically normal human being. In order to learn an ordinary language, such as English, it is necessary to discover how the words that occur in that language pair up with the symbols which are predefined within the language of thought. If users of ordinary language do not display equal degrees of mastery of their language, therefore, that is because some of us have and some of us lack the ingenuity that would be required to discover their correspondence. Our innate knowledge of language is the very same.

When these accounts are reviewed from the perspective of the multiple criteria for scientific theories, it becomes evident that they both encounter the same problem. The experiences "triggering off" recollections may yield learning *without* recollection. The "ingenuity" exercised in discovering correlations might be enough to learn a language *without* an innate language. The theories that Plato and Fodor endorse encompass simpler theories as parts, which do not seem to possess less explanatory and predictive power than do the more complicated theories that contain them. But when this is the case, these more elegant theoretical alternatives ought to be preferred. (We shall return to this issue.)

Plato and Fodor could defend their points of view, of

course, were they in the position to rebut the contention that the systematic power of the contained theories is equal to the systematic power of the theories that contain them. A different approach, which also promises to provide symbols with something to represent, would maintain that the inferential relations that obtain between the various elements of a language is enough to fix what it is that they represent. This view is known as the *inferential network model*.

The inferential network model emphasizes the role of definitions in fixing the meaning of the words that occur in a language. A definition, within this scheme of things, involves two parts—the word, phrase, or expression to be defined (known as the *definiendum*) and the word, phrase, or expression by means of which it is defined (known as the *definiens*). Usually, although not always, the *definiens* is antecedently understood and provides a foundation for understanding the *definiendum*. The *definiens* and the *definiendum* both consist of sequences of symbols (i.e. both of them are linguistic entities).

A typical repository of definitions for an ordinary language with which you are almost certainly familiar is a dictionary for that language. The third edition of *Webster's New World Dictionary* provides definitions such as these:

(D1) bat = df any stout club, stick, or cudgel;
(D2) cat = df a small, lithe, soft-furred animal;
(D3) fat = df fleshy, plump, corpulent, obese.

According to the inferential network model, the occurrence of any of these words (*definienda*) within a sentence could be replaced by their definitions (*definiens*) without loss of meaning, so that if the original sentence was true, the sentence obtained by replacing *definiendum* by *definiens* would be, too.

Whether the inferential network model can possibly salvage the computational conception, however, is highly problematic for at least two reasons. The first is that the computational conception posits an extremely strong relationship between the formal properties of symbol structures and what it is that they represent. The strongest version of this position has it that there is a one-to-one correspondence between symbol structures and what it is they represent. Weaker versions permit many-to-one or one-to-many relations.

In the case of the strongest version, each specific symbol structure may represent one and only one object or property in the world, and each object or property in the world may be represented by one and only one symbol structure. Unfortunately, these hypotheses are not satisfied by an ordinary language, such as English, where the same words can represent more than one object or property in the world. *Webster's* also includes this definition:

(D4) bat = df a furry, nocturnal flying mammal.

Sometimes the word "bat" is used with one of these meanings and sometimes with another. There is no single thing which this word represents in English.

When the same word can be used to stand for more than one thing, it is said to be "ambiguous." The word "bat" stands for more than one thing and is therefore an ambiguous word. When different words can be used to stand for the same thing, they are said to be "synonymous." The *definiens* and the *definiendum* of a proper definition are therefore synonymous. The English language therefore includes words that are ambiguous and words that are synonymous. But that would be impossible if the strongest version of the computational conception were correct. The evidence suggests it is untrue.

The weaker versions of the computational conception maintain *either* that each specific symbol structure represents one and only one object or property in the world *or* that each distinct object or property in the world is represented by one and only one specific symbol structure, *but not both*. The first of these is incompatible with the existence of ambiguous symbols, and the second is incompatible with the existence of synonymous symbols. Hence, either English is not a system of symbols to which the computational conception is intended to apply or else the computational conception is false.

THE PRIMACY OF PRIMITIVES

The argument we have considered supports the conclusion that the computational conception cannot be correct *unless* some other hypothesis could guarantee that symbols (or symbol structures, strings of marks) represent objects and properties in the world. The innate language of thought theory and the inferential network of definitions alternative are not adequate. The evidence suggests that neither of these means can provide a foundation for the computational conception. But perhaps another option has been ignored.

Notice that symbols systems, formal systems, and Turing Machines generate functions that relate symbols (symbol structures, mark sequences) of one kind to symbols (symbol structures, mark sequences) of another. The existence of a function relating one sequence of marks to another sequence of marks does not invariably thereby render either one meaningful. Unless at least some of those symbols stand for something in the world, none of them stands for anything in the world. A mapping from "xyz" onto "123" (or from "123" onto "abc," etc.), by itself, does not render either sequence meaningful.

This point is not difficult to see against the background of the theory of definition. Every word, phrase, or expression that occurs in a language can be defined by means of other words, phrases, or expressions just two ways. First, some words, phrases, or expressions can be defined by means of other words, phrases, or expressions that are eventually defined by means of the originals. Second, new words, phrases, or expressions can be introduced for the purpose of having the same meaning as those old words, phrases, or expressions, where this process of introducing new words must go on forever.

In other words, the only ways to avoid the existence of undefined (or "primitive") words, phrases, and expressions within a language are by resorting to *circular definitions* (ultimately explaining their meaning by referring to those words themselves) or by generating a *definitional regress* (succeeding in attaining the form of definitions but without achieving their purpose). The problem with defining "cognitive science" as "the science of cognition," for example, is that such a definition is circular. The problem with defining "xyz" as "123," "123" as "abc," etc., is that they are all equally meaningless.

Because every defined word, phrase, or expression can be replaced by some word, phrase, or expression by means of which it is defined, every sequence that contains *defined* words, phrases, or expressions can be replaced by another that contains only *undefined* words, phrases, or expressions. The meaning of every word, phrase, or expression in a language is therefore dependent upon the meaning of the primitive words, phrases, or expressions by means of which it is ultimately understood in that language.

The theoretical limitations of the computational conception should now be quite evident. For, without some method that fixes the meaning of the symbols (symbol structures, sequences of marks) that are subject to manipulation, there is no guarantee that any of them represents anything at all. I therefore infer that the primary deficiency of the computational conception is its apparent incapacity to cope with the problem of assigning meaning to the primitive words, phrases, and expressions of the languages it employs.

The objection could be raised on its behalf, no doubt, that even though those symbols (symbol structures, sequences of marks) require interpretation to be meaningful, these interpretations can be supplied by the users of those systems of symbols. The users of those symbol systems, after all, can *interpret* otherwise meaningless symbols (symbol structures, sequences of marks) to stand for objects and properties in the world; "xyz," for example, could stand for three specific persons referred to as "x," "y," and "z," where the same persons are referred to as "1," "2," and "3," by those symbol users.

The problem with this approach may have occurred to you already. It explains the meaning of one sequence of marks ("xyz," say) by appealing to the meaning they possess for *users* of those sequences of marks, without also explaining how *any* sequences of marks stand for anything at all for the *users* themselves. This explanation, in other words, is like the homunculus theory, because it explains the meaning of external marks by reference to the meaning of internal marks, where the meaning of those internal marks is not explained in turn. Apparently "the buck" has been passed once more.

The same result emerges from looking at this problem in three different ways. The first perspective is that of an artificial language in relation to its natural counterpart, where the former is only meant to capture part but not all of the latter. The second is that of higher-level programming languages relative to low-level machine language, where the use of these higher-level languages is convenient, but dispensable, for the purposes of programming machines. The third is that of a language as involving the interpretation of an abstract skeleton of meaningless marks and rules for their manipulation.

First, it is possible to construct an artificial counterpart for a natural language when relevant information is available. This process has been beautifully described by Rudolf Carnap (1881–1970), an important philosopher of science. When the use of language within a community can be subject to observations and experiments (by asking questions, for example), it becomes possible to formulate conjectures concerning what the words stand for and the conditions under which their use would be suitable for various purposes (Carnap, 1939).

It may be necessary to make decisions about the meaning of words that occur in the natural language, for example, if the artificial counterpart is intended to differ from it by eliminating words with more than one meaning. Whether the word "bat" should occur with the same meaning as (D1) or the same meaning as (D4) might have to be determined. Other decisions would also have to be made concerning synonymous expressions, etc. The important point is that the meaning of the words that occur in a language like this depends upon the meaning of the words that occur in its natural counterpart.

Second, high-level programming languages are commonly employed for the purpose of conveying instructions to computers. The machines operate on the basis of machine language, which consists of sequences of 0's and 1's (of high and low voltage), in accordance with the same principles that obtain for Universal Turing Machines. These high-level languages, including Pascal, Prolog, and Lisp, simulate abstract machines whose instructions can be more readily composed than can those of the target machines that execute them.

If we distinguish between the "data" processed by the machine (its "inputs" and its "outputs") as opposed to the operations that it performs on the data, it turns out that the capacity of the machine to process the data is not determined by what that data stands for in the world (if it "stands for" anything at all). The meaning of the computer commands that are expressed in a high-level programming language, however, depends upon the operations for which they stand in machine language. Once again, we discover that the meaning of a language turns out to be a function of the meaning of another.

Third, the theory of formal systems, including the philosophy of mathematics, draws a crucial distinction between interpreted and uninterpreted formal systems. The formal properties of a symbol system, you may recall, include the shapes, the sizes, and the relative locations of the marks that are the elements of that system. The points, lines, and figures employed in solid geometry are useful illustrations, where the points, lines, and figures that are subject to manipulation can be viewed either as meaningless marks that have no physical counterparts or else as meaningful marks that do.

When lines are identified with paths of light rays in space, points with the intersection of those rays, and figures with the portions of space that they inscribe, the status of the theorems that are validly derived from the axioms of solid geometry undergoes an important alteration. The truth of those theorems is no longer merely a question of whether or not they have been derived from those axioms in accordance with the relevant principles of inference. It becomes significant to ask whether or not the world corresponds to the descriptions provided by those theorems, which might be false.

The parallels are notable. An artificial language consists of a system of elements whose meaning depends upon those of some ordinary language. A programming language is a system of elements that represent something in the world only if those of another language do. A formal system consists of a system of elements that stand for something in the world provided they are subject to an appropriate interpretation. None of the elements of these systems possesses any meaning apart from the meaning of their primitives. What we do not yet understand is how these primitives can have meaning.

CAUSAL THEORIES OF REFERENCE

At least one alternative that might be thought to defeat this critique of computational conceptions deserves consideration here. A great deal of excitement has been generated in recent times by what has come to be known as "the causal theory of reference." First introduced by Saul Kripke, a well-known American philosopher, this theory suggests that names acquire their reference (what they stand for) by virtue of causal relations that obtain between someone learning that name and the something that bears that name.

The general idea is that if you were to meet me on some specific occasion, say, after a public lecture I presented on minds and machines, then the reference of the name "James H. Fetzer" would be fixed by the causal relation in which we stood at that moment in time, say, when we shook hands. You would know thereafter that the thing you refer to by that name was the same thing with which you shook hands on that specific occasion. The reference of "James H. Fetzer" would thereby have been permanently fixed.

A problem with this view, I think, is that innumerable specific features are present on any such occasion that should not be relevant to reference. The room in which we met, for example, was of a certain size and decor, and I was wearing a particular jacket and trousers. That was the thing to which you stood in a specific causal relation. So when I am no longer in that room or have changed my jacket, to what does the name "James H. Fetzer" refer? The causal theory of names seems to provide no resolution of this difficulty.

This approach can be extended to cover predicate expressions (such as common nouns and adjectives) as well as proper names. In Chapter 2, for example, during our discussion of the hypothesis that we might be nothing more than brains in vats, we encountered the idea that the meaning of our thoughts of *apple trees* might be in the world rather than in our heads. If meanings depend upon causal connections between minds or their contents and things that exist in the world, such as apple trees, then there *is* a sense in which meanings are in the world rather than in our heads. The appearance of apple trees, for example, might bring about thoughts of apple trees.

Several other problems affect theories of this general kind, which are today widely embraced. One is that they violate the traditional distinction between intension and extension. The *intension* of a term (a word, phrase or whatever) is the conditions that must be satisfied for that term to apply to something. The intension of "chair", for example, might be specified as a raised surface suitable for sitting by one person, which is (usually) easily movable. The intension of a term, in general, thus corresponds to its definiens. The *extension* of a term, by contrast, is the set of things (past, present or future) that satisfy those conditions. In this case, that would include all things of that kind—lawn chairs, desk chairs, office chairs, etc.—in the world.

Causal theories of reference attempt to solve the problem of meaning by making extensions the *meaning* of words, phrases and expressions. No one would want to deny that an approach of this kind possesses a certain superficial plausibility. Who would want to deny, for example, that apple trees within a suitable causal proximity tend to bring about thoughts that relate to apple trees for those who possess the concept? The problem this approach encounters is that the kinds of cases it takes to be illustrative of meaning relations are special cases that do not seem to be representative.

Consider, for example, that causal theories of reference take for granted the possibility of a causal relationship between those things by means of which we think (call them *thought-tokens*) and those things for which thought-tokens stand (call them *token-things*). If token-things could not stand in causal relations to corresponding thought-tokens, those thought-tokens could not possibly stand for them. Corresponding thought-tokens would be unable to have those token-things as their meaning, since there would be no causal connection to infuse the thought-tokens with meaning.

When we consider a broader range of thought-tokens than those that motivate causal theories of reference, however, this approach appears to encounter insuperable obstacles. The thought-tokens that we employ include those that stand for *non-existent things* (whether werewolves and vampires, in the case of predicates, or Santa Claus and Mary Poppins, in the case of proper names). Other stand for *abstract objects* (such as pi and the square-root of -1), *theoretical properties* (such as gravitational attractions and electromagnetic forces), and *non-observable properties* (such as conductivity, malleability, etc., as well as motives and beliefs). None of these token-things stand in obvious causal relations to their thought-tokens.

When advocates of computational conceptions suggest that the problem of meaning can be solved on the basis of the causal theory of reference, the proper attitude to adopt ought to be one of skepticism. There may be something to causal theories, but what there is remains to be seen. Indeed, if the solution to the problem of meaning advanced in the following chapters turns out to be right, then causal theories are wrong. At the very least, a correct account of meaning appears to require an approach of a very different kind.

CHAPTER FIVE

WHAT IS MENTALITY?

INTENSIONALITY

Among the most important words that have functioned as primitive (or "undefined") words during the last several chapters of this book are "represents," "stands for," and "means." All of these words concern a relationship that may obtain between a thing x and a thing y when x represents, stands for, or means y. We now know that definitional relationships are one of the ways in which a linguistic entity, word $w1$, can represent, stand for, or mean another linguistic entity, word $w2$. What we don't know is how any undefined (or "primitive") word can possibly represent, stand for, or mean anything.

If we knew how natural languages acquire their meaning, we could explain how artificial languages capture part but not all of their meaning, too. If we knew how machine language possesses its meaning, we could explain how higher-level programming languages acquire their meaning. And if we knew how formal systems can be interpreted to apply to things in the world, we could understand the difference between pure and applied mathematics. Solutions to any of these problems might resolve them all. For openers, let's explore the nature of ordinary languages more closely than we have before.

Ordinary languages may be viewed as having three kinds of properties. The first kind are their *syntactical* properties, which correspond to the formal properties of the elements of those languages and the rules by means of which sentences can be created out of them. The second kind are their *semantical* properties, which correspond to the relations between words and sentences and what they represent, stand for, or mean. The third kind are their *pragmatical* properties, which correspond to the relations that may obtain between elements of those languages, what they mean, and their users.

Our exploration of the computational conception of language and mentality can now be described from another point of view. Since it is essential to the computational conception that operations on symbols are purely formal, the only features of an ordinary language that are accessible to computational procedures are its purely formal (or "syntactical") properties. Since these purely formal properties do not encompass the semantical properties of an ordinary language, it should be obvious why a computational conception encounters the problem of representation. It lacks the resources to resolve it.

The reason why the hypothesis of the language of thought, on the one hand, and the inferential network model, on the other, are so important for the potential defense of the computational conception should now be quite clear. They afford an avenue for infusing formal properties with semantic content. Without some means for securing an appropriate relationship between the syntactical properties it can handle and the semantical properties it cannot, the computational conception loses its plausibility. It no more resembles any ordinary language than does an uninterpreted formal system.

The language of thought hypothesis, moreover, is too strong, while the inferential network model is too weak. The language of thought hypothesis would have us believe that every neurologically normal human brain comes with every primitive semantic distinction that we could ever need "built in" from conception. The inferential network model would have us believe that functions relating possibly meaningless sequences of marks to other possibly meaningless sequences of marks could be enough to render either sequence meaningful.

If there is a solution to this problem, it lies in another direction.

Indeed, the difficulty we are encountering here has been dealt with by philosophers in the past. The problem of establishing how the primitive elements of a system possess any meaning has been referred to as the problem of *primitive intensionality*, while the problem of establishing how the defined elements of a system possess their meaning has been referred to as the problem of *derivative intensionality*. Almost everyone would agree, I think, that the problem of derivative intensionality becomes trivial when the problem of primitive intensionality has been solved. The problem is to solve it.

INTENSIONAL CONTEXTS

Before pursuing this issue further, however, we need to review some of the distinctions that are important to its consideration. This section will be somewhat more technical than most of the other sections of this book, but at times there is no choice. Either we draw the distinctions that we need to understand a problem (in which case, we understand it better with a little effort) or we don't draw the distinctions that we need to understand a problem (in which case, we conserve our effort at the cost of our understanding).

We already know that ordinary languages consist of a vocabulary and a grammar. We know that the vocabulary of those languages consists of some defined words and some undefined words and that every defined word can, in principle, be replaced by some sequence of undefined words without any loss of meaning. The words that compose their vocabularies, of course, consist of proper nouns, pronouns, common nouns, and adjectives, which can be used to name (proper nouns and pronouns) and to describe (common nouns and adjectives) specific things and kinds of things that may be in the world.

In addition to these words (which can be used to name and to describe), other words are also found in ordinary languages that serve different functions. The word "is," for example, occurs as an *assertion of identity* (when someone referred to by a specific name is said to be the same person as the person referred to by a unique description, such as, say, "Mike Tyson is the heavyweight boxing champion of the world"). But "is" also occurs as a *mode of predication* (when something referred to by a specific name or a description is said to have a specific property, such as "Mike Tyson is a millionaire," which is not unique.)

While the word "is" and its variants, such as "are," can occur in a variety of tenses (past, present, and future, for example), they always occur as part of the internal structure of specific sentences. Other words create new sentences out of old, where these include "if . . . then —," ". . . and —," and ". . . or —." Given two sequences of marks that qualify as sentences of a language, just as "Grass is green" and "Snow is white" qualify as sentences of English, these words can generate "If grass is green, then snow is white," "Grass is green, and snow is white" or "Grass is green or snow is white," for example.

These distinctions have been refined by philosophers and linguists, but here these should suffice. If we refer to the naming expressions and the descriptive expressions of a language as its *descriptive vocabulary* and to the means by which various sentences can be formed and new sentences can be fashioned out of them as its *logical vocabulary*, then the descriptive vocabulary and the logical vocabulary constitute the vocabulary of an ordinary language. The rules by which the elements of this vocabulary can be combined to create both singular and general sentences are called its *formation rules*.

The subject known as "logic" is concerned with the nature of arguments. There are two kinds of logic, deductive and inductive, which we are going to investigate further in Chapters 7 and 8. For the moment, it is enough to note that students of logic have realized for some time that there are at least two kinds of sentences that are built-up out of other sentences. There are those whose *truth-value* (true, false) is completely determined by the truth-values of those sentences from which they are built and others that are not. Those of the first kind are called *truth-functional*, the second *non-truth-functional*.

Consider, for example, the sentence "Grass is green, and snow is white." This sentence, of course, is built up out of two component sentences, "Grass is green" and "Snow is white." The sentence that results from joining them together by means of an ". . . and —" connective (where one sentence occupies the ". . . " position and another the "—" position) is known as a conjunction. A conjunction is truth-functional when the truth-value of the conjunction is completely determined by the truth-values of its two conjuncts. Such a sentence is true when and only when both its conjuncts happen to be true.

The example we have considered is a truth-functional sentence. Consider now two other sentences, "Mary got married" and "Mary had a baby." We may initially suppose that the conjunction of these two sentences would also be truth-functional. But consider the example. "Mary got married, and Mary had a baby" says one thing in ordinary language, whereas "Mary had a baby, and Mary got married" says another. Hence, a sentence of the form ". . . and —" in ordinary language is sometimes truth-functional but sometimes not.

This specific kind of non-truth-functionality is not especially interesting, because it is not difficult to understand. The use of ". . . and —" in English sometimes involves a temporal aspect but sometimes not. Sometimes, that is, the event, occurrence, or state of affairs described by the first sentence is supposed to occur *earlier than* the event, occurrence, or state of affairs described by the second. When this occurs within an ordinary language context, the translation of that sentence using a truth-functional connective must fail.

Indeed, this is one of the reasons why an artificial language can capture part but not all of its ordinary language counterpart. Attempts to codify, to regularize, or to standardize the use of a language involves the codification, regularization, or standardization of multiply ambiguous words, where what they are intended to represent, stand for, or mean within a specific communication situation tends to be resolved by contextual cues. They may involve prior information, knowledge, and beliefs shared by the participants in that exchange. These can disappear in the construction of an artificial language.

The phrase "It is not the case that —" is another example of a truth-functional operator, since the truth-value of the sentence that results from its application reverses the truth-value of the original. If the sentence "It is raining outside" happens to be true, then the truth-value of the sentence "It is not the case that it is raining outside" must be the opposite (i.e. false). But there are other operators that, when applied to sentences that are true, yield sentences whose truth-values are not determined by that truth-value.

An especially important kind of non-truth-functionality that can occur in ordinary language takes place in relation to states of information, knowledge, and belief. Consider the phrases "Harry knows that —," "Joan thinks that —," and "Bill doubts that —." These are operators that create a new sentence when they are applied to an old sentence. Yet the truth-values of these new sentences is not determined by the truth-values of the sentences to which they are applied. These sentences are interesting, because in some sense this phenomenon arises because we have tacitly changed the subject.

Just because the sentence "A lunar eclipse occurred the night of 16 August 1989" might be true does not dictate that the sentences "Harry knows that a lunar eclipse occurred the night of 16 August 1989," "Joan thinks that a lunar eclipse occurred the night of 16 August 1989," etc., must also be true. The application of these operators to this sentence has changed the subject from an eclipse of the moon on a certain occasion to what Harry knows, Joan thinks, etc. Their content has shifted from a lunar event to a state of mind.

These examples illustrate one species of a broader genus that is often referred to as *intensional contexts*. These contexts are symptomatic of, but do not exhaust, the manifestations associated with the phenomena that accompany the use of something (such as symbols, words, or sentences) to stand for something else (such as a person, event, or state of affairs). One way to consider what they involve is to realize that the use of language to describe things (as an example of intensionality) often brings with it the consequence that we understand what we understand in relation to specific descriptions.

Perhaps the key to understanding this issue is that the descriptions that we use to describe and to refer to things in the world (including people and places) tend to describe only *some* of their properties. It might be true that you were the first baby born after midnight at the hospital where you were born, but that is hardly the *only* property that you possess. You have lived in various locations at various times, you have specific family members and relatives, you have accomplished some feats and failed to accomplish others. While you might satisfy the description of being "the first baby born after midnight," etc., numerous other descriptions are also (uniquely) true of you.

Suppose, for example, that your mother knows that you were the first baby born after midnight at your hospital. She might not know other things that are true of you. Perhaps you forgot to mention that you were chosen to take the lead in the class play. Indeed, even if you had mentioned it to her, she might not have realized that the first person born after midnight at your hospital has been chosen to take the lead in the class play. These things are true of you, but they may be things that your mother either does not know or has not yet put together. Sometimes we are disappointed when our parents do not put things together, of course, but other times we are relieved.

There is something about examples like these that philosophers have found to be revealing about the nature of intensionality. It has to do with the "aboutness" of the relations that obtain when one thing represents another. It has to do with referring to objects, events, and states of affairs by means of descriptions. The problems we have reviewed have involved assertions of identity and modes of predication that occur within ordinary language. But intensionality is broader than this. If we are going to understand its nature, we are going to have to go beyond the confines of language.

SEMIOTIC SYSTEMS

The idea of going beyond the confines of language to understand the nature of intensionality may strike you as odd, especially if you are inclined to suppose that thought presupposes language because all thinking takes place in language. How could we then "go beyond" the confines of language? Yet you have almost certainly heard the expression "A picture is worth a thousand words." If you now pause and think about it, it might occur to you that words are elements of language, while pictures—at least, ordinary pictures as opposed to hieroglyphics—are not. That should raise the glimmer of possibility that maybe there is something more to thinking than language alone.

The United States has not produced a large number of important philosophers (by which I mean philosophers who really are important rather than those who think they are), but one figure about whom there is no doubt was named Charles S. Peirce (1839–1914). Peirce advanced a theory that invites us to encompass sights and sounds as well as words and sentences among all the kinds of things that can be elements of thoughts. The foundation for the theory he advanced is the notion of a *sign*, where a sign is understood to be a something that stands for something (else) in some respect or other for somebody (Peirce, 1897). This is one of the most important ideas we will encounter in this book.

Notice several features of Peirce's conception. A sign is a

something (so it exists in the world) that stands for something (which might be itself or another thing) *in some respect or other*. That it stands for something "in some respect or other" should have the right ring to you, because this is the aspect of intensionality that we have been discussing, namely, that you can refer to something on the basis of some of its properties without mentioning, implying, or otherwise referring to its other properties at all. That a sign is a something that stands for something (else) in some respect or other *for somebody* is also worth emphasizing, because this feature of Peirce's analysis makes it a pragmatic account. The users of signs are essential to this theory of signs.

Peirce distinguished three kinds of signs based upon the different ways in which signs of those kinds "stand for" that for which they stand. The first kind of sign that he identified are those that stand for (other) things because they *resemble* those (other) things in some respect or other. Pictures, photographs, and statues are typical examples of signs of this kind, to which Peirce gave the name "icons." What is most important to notice about icons, I think, is that the respects in which something may resemble something (else) tends to presuppose a point of view. Your driver's license photograph, for example, may look like you (on a bad day) when viewed from face forward, but not if viewed from the side (you are just not that thin!). It stands for you because it resembles you and you resemble it when you adopt the right point of view.

The second kind of sign that Peirce identified consists of signs that stand for (other) things because they are *causes or effects* of those (other) things in some respect or other. The ashes that remain from a fire and the smoke that it produces are both examples of signs of this kind, to which Peirce gave the name "indices." The symptoms of a disease, such as the red spots and elevated temperature that accompanies the measles, are typical indices in Peirce's sense. Notice that even these signs stand for that for which they stand only in certain specific respects. Smoke stands for a fire as an effect of a fire, but smoke alone does not indicate the size of the fire, the material that is aflame, or the harm to the environment that may accrue from an event of that kind.

The third kind of sign that Peirce identified consists of signs that stand for (other) things because they are *habitually associated* with those (other) things in some respect or other. The words and sentences that occur in any ordinary language, for example, are signs of this kind, to which Peirce gave the name "symbols." The words "chair," "horse," and "dime" are typical examples of symbols in Peirce's sense. Notice, in particular, that these words consist of certain letters in a certain sequence, whereas the things for which they stand consist of things upon which one might sit (chairs), that romp around in fields (horses), or that one might spend (dimes). These signs neither resemble nor are causes or effects of those things for which they stand.

To appreciate the difference between signs of these kinds, observe that relations of resemblance and of cause and effect are there in the world whether we notice them or not, whereas habitual associations have to be acquired. This means that icons and indices stand for that for which they stand as a result of relations between those things that are natural. They exist in nature (between those things) whether we notice them or not. Symbols, however, only stand for that for which they stand as a result of their association by sign users. When symbols are used by a small group or by just one person, they must be adopted, invented, or created by the users of those signs.

This point deserves elaboration. In order for any sign (no matter whether icon, index, or symbol) to stand for something (else) in some respect or other *for somebody*, some relation between that something and that something (else)—between the sign and that for which it stands—must obtain on the part of its user. This connection could be based on a relation of resemblance, of cause or effect, or of habitual association, as we have discovered. Without the existence of such a connection between that sign and that for which it stands by such a user, it would not be the case that the sign stands for something (else) in some respect or other for somebody (or thing) at all.

For the purpose of our inquiry, the most striking feature of Peirce's theory of signs is that it suggests a corresponding theory of minds, according to which *minds* are sign-using (or "semiotic") systems. This approach has been proposed by the author of this book (Fetzer, 1988, 1989, 1990). From this perspective, Peirce's conception should be broadened in the following respect. A sign should be a something that stands for something (else) in some respect or other *for something*. This makes it clear that those things for which something can stand for something (else) might be human, other animal, or machine, without tacitly hinting that the kind of thing for which something can stand for something (else) must be something *human*. It allows the possibility that other animals and machines might have minds.

Before turning to some of the ramifications of this conception of minds as semiotic systems, it might be a good idea to pause to consider the use of the word "symbol" and of the phrase "symbol system." In Chapter 4, these words and phrases were used to describe the physical patterns that can occur as elements of another type of entity called a "symbol structure" and to describe a special kind of Turing Machine that can manipulate those strings. It is extremely important to recognize that, although Peirce and Newell and Simon use similar terms, they occur with very different senses. The differences between them, moreover, appear to be exactly those differences that distinguish between mere computational machines and real thinking things.

MODES OF MENTALITY

One of the most intriguing ramifications of a theory of mind based upon Peirce's theory of signs is its suggestive (or "heuristic") fertility in indicating that there may be several species of mentality rather than simply one. Thus, if some signs are icons, other signs are indices, and still others are symbols, it is not difficult to imagine that there might be corresponding types of minds, where some minds can use icons, other minds can use indices, and still other minds can use symbols. The conception of minds as sign-using systems thus suggests in turn the prospect of differentiating minds of Type I (as systems that can use icons), minds of Type II (as systems that can use indices), and minds of Type III (as systems that can use symbols) as three kinds of minds.

This account is reinforced by the realization that these three types also appear to reflect successively stronger and stronger kinds of minds. Notice, especially, that the use of indices seems to presuppose the use of icons (since the use of indices appears to presuppose the capacity to respond to different instances of causes and effects as instances of the same kind on the basis of resemblance relations). The use of symbols, moreover, seems to presuppose the use of indices (since the use of symbols appears to presuppose the capacity to respond to different instances of signs as causes or effects, even when they function as causes or effects of human behavior on the basis of habitual connections). There thus seems to be a hierarchy of types of mentality here.

One of the fascinating features of this approach is that it supplies a criterion of mentality in the form of the capacity to make a mistake. After all, if something has *the capacity to make a mistake* (i.e. to mis-take something as standing for something other than that for which it stands), it must have the ability to take something *x* to stand for something *y* in some respect or other, which is the right result. This general criterion can be supplemented by other (more specific) criteria in the case of each of these three types of mentality. This account of mentality, moreover, is applicable to humans, to other animals, and to machines alike, since what it takes to be a mind is to have the capacity to utilize signs. Whatever can do that has (or is) a mind.

Consider, for example, the following case as an illustration of semiotic systems of Type I. A recent article, entitled "Fake Owls Chase Away Pests," appeared in the newspaper *The St. Petersburg Times* on 27 January 1986:

Birds may fly over the rainbow, but until 10 days ago, many of them chose to roost on top of a billboard that hangs over Bill Allen's used car lot on Drew Street in Clearwater. Allen said he tried everything he could think of to scare away the birds, but still they came— sometimes as many as 100 at a time. He said an employee had to wash the used cars at Royal Auto Sales every day to clean off the birds' droppings. About a month ago, Allen said, he called the billboard's owner for help fighting the birds. Shortly afterward, Allen said, two vinyl owl "look alikes" were put on the corners of the billboard. "I haven't had a bird land up there since," he said.

The birds, in other words, took the shapes and sizes of the vinyl owls to be instances of the shapes and sizes of the real thing. The birds mistook the fake owls for real owls, which is a special case of mistaking the false for the true.

The phenomenon of mistaking a resemblance relationship of one kind for a resemblance relationship of another kind, of course, is not unfamiliar to the law enforcement agencies of federal and state governments. The benefits of counterfeiting money, for example, derive from creating products that look like the real thing but that were created by a different process. There was a time when false fannies and other enhancements were popular among the young and even the not-so-young people of this country, precisely because they created the impression of possessing physical attributes that were supposed to be desirable to members of the opposite sex. False teeth and fake diplomas are other examples among effective illusions. You do not want to draw the inference that mistakes of this kind are strictly for the birds.

Consider the following familiar case as an example of

semiotic systems of Type II. During his experiments with dogs, Ivan Pavlov (1849–1936), a great Russian physiologist, discovered the phenomenon known as *classical conditioning*. This occurs when a cause that usually brings about a certain effect for a specific organism is paired up with another stimulus that usually does not bring about that effect. A dog that would ordinarily salivate at the sight of its food but not at the sound of a bell, for example, could be conditioned to salivate at the sound of a bell as well, if the bell were sounded in suitable proximity to the presentation of food according to a certain schedule.

Pavlov found that if this second stimulus (called the "conditioned" stimulus) were paired up appropriately with the first (called the "unconditioned" stimulus), then it would tend to become a productive stimulus with respect to the original effect. Dogs that salivated at the sound of the bell, therefore, were taking such a sound as an indication of the immediate satiation of their hunger just as they were taking the sight of their food as an indication of the immediate satiation of their hunger. The food itself, however, would be the cause of hunger satiation, once it were consumed, because food has the tendency to satiate hunger. But the bell could never be the cause of hunger satiation, once it were heard, because such things do not tend to satiate hunger.

And consider the following case as an illustration of semiotic systems of Type III. The influential behaviorist B. F. Skinner, whom we encountered in Chapter 1, has conducted numerous experiments with pigeons and with rats. During the course of his research, Skinner discovered the phenomenon which is known as *operant conditioning*. Operant conditioning occurs when a class, kind, or type of behavior that an organism has displayed more or less at random is selectively reinforced. Skinner discovered that by providing a positive form of reinforcement on an appropriate schedule he could increase the frequency with which certain behaviors are displayed, and that by providing a negative form of reinforcement on a similar schedule he could decrease it.

A pigeon in a experimental apparatus (now known as a "Skinner box"), for example, could be subjected to conditions in which pressing a bar would cause a food pellet to be released when a green light was on but otherwise not. The pigeon might then press the bar when the light was on in the expectation of receiving food, only to be disappointed when it did not happen (because, say, Skinner's graduate assistant forgot to refill the pellet supply). In such a case, the pigeon would have mistaken a method of obtaining food that has worked in the past for a method of obtaining food that would work in the future. Since the problem of when inferences about the future are justified on the basis of experience about the past is known as "the problem of induction," the pigeon may be said to have encountered the problem of induction.

No doubt, there is plenty of room to debate these examples. The case of the fake owls, for example, could be said to exhibit indexical mentality along with iconic mentality, since it was the effect of being killed by real owls that the birds wanted to avoid. Nevertheless, it was the resemblance relation of the fake owls to the real thing that brought about this response. Similarly, it could be claimed that Pavlov's experiments reflect symbolic mentality no less than Skinner's. This is an extremely interesting question, because it tends to test the adequacy of the classification scheme for types of mentality that is a consequence of the conception of minds as semiotic systems. It might be a worthwhile exercise to debate their similarities and differences during class.

It should be borne in mind, however, that the distinction between minds of these three kinds rests upon the manner in which the signs they can utilize are related to that for which they can stand. In all three cases, it must be possible for signs of these kinds—icons, indices, and symbols alike—to stand in a causal relation to sign users. The fact that the presence of a sign of one of these kinds exerts a causal influence upon its user makes no difference to the kind of sign that a sign happens to be. It would also be a wrong to overlook the basic difference between classical and operant conditioning. Both involve relating presumptive causes with their expected effects. The difference is that, in Skinner's case, behavior is reinforced after it has been displayed, where organisms tend to acquire the capacity of adopting means appropriate to their desired ends—which is not the case for Pavlov's subjects.

HIGHER TYPES OF MENTALITY

It is fascinating to consider whether there could be even higher types of mentality than those of Type III. One possibility might be reflected by a capacity for utilizing arrangements of symbols for the purpose of constructing arguments. In this case, some of those symbols would function as premises by providing the grounds, reasons, or evidence for other symbols as conclusions. This suggestion has been advanced by Sir Karl Popper, whose methodology of corroboration was introduced in Chapter 1. Popper (1982), in fact, offers a conception of four levels of function of language, including an expressive function (of animals and plants), a signal function (of some animals, including bees), a descriptive function (especially of humans), and an argumentative function. Popper's theory affords an interesting contrast to mine.

It is unnecessary to convert to Popper's conception, however, merely to appreciate the contribution that it might make to the approach that is being pursued here. The recognition of an argumentative capacity as a higher type of mentality than Type III suggests that an appropriate criterion for mentality of this kind would be the capacity for logical reasoning. The standards of reasoning that are established by logic, after all, indicate the conditions under which specific conclusions are supported by specific premises (either conclusively, as in the case of deductive reasoning; or inconclusively, as in the case of inductive reasoning). Either way, the ability to satisfy the normative requirements specified by appropriate principles of logic would seem to afford a reliable evidential indicator that a system possesses this level of mentality.

I shall therefore assume that semiotic systems that are capable of argumentative reasoning display mentality of Type IV, a criterion of which is the capacity for logical reasoning. Yet there appears to be an even higher level of mental functioning, namely, metamentality, in which signs are used to stand for other signs. The criterion for mentality of this level, moreover, appears to be the capacity for criticism. When a critic takes to task a film, a play, a book or whatever, he is engaging in an activity in which signs are used to stand for other signs. Films, plays, books, and the like, after all, have their own distinctive modes of signification, whereby they stand for that for which they stand in relation to various levels of interpretation (which are also points of view).

Indeed, the Popperian spirit infuses the process of criticism, for Popper especially has championed the idea of conjectures and attempted refutations, of thinking things through and of killing our ideas instead of ourselves—ideas with important evolutionary ramifications (Popper, 1978). The function of criticism tends to be to attempt to determine whether some specific purpose for behavior or some specific use of signs might have been better achieved by various other arrangements (of deeds or of words, etc.) than those that were in fact employed. Especially important examples of criticism appear to be those involved in planning for the future (by individuals, by groups, or by societies). Reaching decisions that affect what will happen to us may be the most consequential activity in which human beings engage, since they tend to affect the prospects for the evolution and survival of our species.

For these and other reasons, it appears to be appropriate to acknowledge that semiotic systems that are capable of metamentality display mentality of Type V, a criterion of which is the capacity for criticism. The theory of mind that I have elaborated on the basis of Peirce's theory of signs, at least in general, appears to be sufficiently rich and varied to accommodate a wide range of phenomena that might be viewed as involving aspects of mentality. It is not the only possible approach, however, since Popper (1978, 1982) and Dretske (1981, 1988), among others, have offered differing accounts. I think that the theory of minds as semiotic systems is superior to all of its alternatives, but this is not something that I have sought to establish here.

Indeed, an evaluation of the relative virtues of these distinct philosophical theories is even more troublesome than is an assessment of the comparative merits of alternative scientific theories. The multiple criteria that are relevant for the evaluation of scientific theories were introduced in Chapter 1. The corresponding criteria which are relevant for the comparison of philosophical theories are somewhat more difficult to specify, because these theories have the character of *recommendations* (or "proposals"), which cannot be regarded as simply "true" or "false." Instead, as Hempel (1952) suggests, their relative adequacy may be measured on the basis of the extent to which they tend to clarify and illuminate conceptual and theoretical problems that have resisted previous efforts to resolve them. From this point of view, the solutions I am advancing here represent invitations to further investigation.

The purpose of this book, as the Preface has explained, is to isolate and identify the principal philosophical difficulties that cognitive science encounters. Its aim is to discover why cognitive science is necessary—if it is necessary—and how it is possible—if it is possible. One purpose of this chapter has been to establish that a theory of the mind is not impossible by elaborating the promising conception of minds as semiotic systems. Another purpose of this chapter (and the last) has been to establish that computational and representational conceptions of language and mentality are theoretically inadequate. The purpose of these chapters will therefore have been fulfilled as long as you are convinced that adequate conceptions language and mentality cannot be computational or representational in kind. So if you still have any doubts on this score, it might be appropriate to review Chapters 4 and 5 once more.

CHAPTER SIX

CONNECTIONISM AND COGNITION

A DISPOSITIONAL CONCEPTION

A theory of minds as semiotic systems and even a classification of types of minds on the basis of the kinds of signs they have the capacity to utilize is all very well, you may be thinking, but it still does not explain how *any* sign can be significant for *any* user at all. The distinctions that have been drawn in Chapter 5, after all, are principally semantical in characterizing different ways in which something can stand for something (else) by virtue of one or another kind of relationship (of resemblance, of cause or effect, or of habitual association) between those signs and those things for those sign users. It still does not explain how any signs of any of these kinds can be meaningful for sign users. It does not yet account for the meaning of primitive signs.

This objection can be formulated a different way, but it has the same result. One aspect of the discussion of Chapter 4 was that neither the language of thought hypothesis nor the inferential network conception were successful in accounting for the meaning of primitive words within a language. What is now evident is that a theory of mind based upon Peirce's theory of signs encounters a similar obligation, namely, to explain exactly how the primitive elements of a system of signs can be meaningful for a user of signs (a mind). Otherwise, it would be a mistake to contend—as implicitly I have been doing—that the theory of minds as semiotic systems improves upon such accounts.

The solution to this crucial problem was anticipated by Peirce when he observed that "the most perfect account of a concept that words can convey will consist of a description of the habit which that concept is calculated to produce" (Peirce, 1906, p. 286). This suggests the possibility that the meaning of primitive signs might be grounded in the habits, tendencies, and dispositions to which they give rise. An account of this kind falls within what has come to be known as *functionalist conceptions* of language and mentality, because it characterizes the meaning of primitives by means of the causal role that they play in affecting behavior. It goes beyond other functionalist conceptions in the specific role it assigns to habits, tendencies, and dispositions.

An alternative to Fodor's theory of learning a language, from this point of view, would be to assume that learning does involve acquiring some kind of "understanding" without presuming that the kind of understanding that is involved here has to be *linguistic*. As infants and children, we usually learn to do things (drink from a bottle, play with toys, scribble and draw) without having any names or labels for the activities thereby performed. It should not be especially surprising, therefore, that when initially unfamiliar words are associated with already familiar things, including particular patterns of behavior that we have already displayed, it does not demand extraordinary ingenuity or vast experience for any neurologically normal human being to learn forms of language that are appropriate to their age and past experience.

We seldom think about defining words like "wood," "hammer," and "nail," because we can use them (and can know how to use them) without the intervention of other linguistic forms. With respect to the primitive terms that occur in any ordinary language (or the primitive signs that occur in any system of signs), we must discover how they are used rather than ask for their linguistic meaning. Indeed, this view was championed by Ludwig Wittgenstein (1889–1951), one of the most influential of all twentieth-century philosophers, in what is now referred to as his later work. From this perspective, knowledge of language is far more adequately envisioned as a *skill* than as a *state* (as a matter of "knowing how" rather than of "knowing that"). This may be the essential misconception lying at the foundation of nonpragmatical accounts.

There thus appear to be at least three different ways in which a syntax (grammar) might be supposed to be infused with meaning (semantics). One would be to suggest that every neurologically normal human being is born a speaker of a specific language. The existence of ordinary languages, such as French, German, and Russian, with such different grammars and vocabularies makes that hypothesis very hard to swallow. Indeed, Chinese children who have been raised in America grow up speaking English, and American children who have been raised in China grow up speaking Chinese. There seems to be little reason to suppose that this fanciful thesis could possibly be true.

A second would be to concede that, while it is clearly not the case that every neurologically normal human being is born a speaker of a specific language, nevertheless, every neurologically normal human being is born with an innate mental language. The connections that obtain between this innate mental language and an ordinary language have to be learned by discovering a correlation between the linguistic primitives of that ordinary language and the psychological primitives of the innate mental language. Fodor's account, of course, is one of this kind, where theories of both of these kinds maintain that the specific primitives we use is determined as a matter of natural law.

A third would be to deny that there exist laws of nature of either kind, namely, those that genetically determine the specific language that anyone speaks and those that genetically determine the specific primitives that anyone can employ. A theory of this kind asserts that these connections have to be established either by habit (for sign users individually) or by convention (for sign users collectively). Only a theory of this kind offers the promise of resolving the difficulties that are encountered by theories of the other kinds. Moreover, it also offers the prospect of explaining the connections that obtain between the intensional properties of language and their causal capabilities.

The crucial problem that must be solved is to explain how the theory of signs can provide a foundation for systematically explaining and predicting the behavior of sign users. During the course of these explorations, we have encountered the idea that human behavior—at least, when it is voluntary—tends to be brought about by a specific individual's motives and beliefs. The difficulty that has to be resolved in order for the theory of minds as semiotic systems to contribute to understanding human behavior, therefore, is that of accounting for the role of signs as causal determinants of human behavior. A successful analysis might be extended to other animals or even to machines.

CONCEPTS AND COGNITION

The theory of signs provides a foundation for the theory of belief only if what we shall call a *theory of cognition* ties them together. While signs provide modes of reference for objects and for properties, they lack the assertive character of beliefs and sentences (i.e. they are not either true or false). The connection between signs and beliefs for a semiotic system appears to be a causal process that arises when a system becomes conscious of a sign in relation to its *other internal states*, including its preexisting motives and beliefs. When such a system becomes conscious of something that functions as a sign for that system, its cognitive significance results from causal interaction between its awareness of that sign and its *context* (other internal states).

The use of the term "conscious" deserves some elaboration

here, since I do not intend to suggest thereby that every sign user is able to articulate the influence of every sign that influences it at every moment it endures. All of us tend to be affected by the presence or absence of innumerable signs that make a difference to our behavior but whose presence or absence is not anything we could readily put into words. Consider, for example, all of the environmental cues that indicate to us when it is appropriate to pass another car when we are driving along a highway. The weather, the time of day, traffic conditions, and the like all exert their subtle influence, but we might be hard pressed to express in language every factor that affects what we actually do.

The term "conscious" can even be defined for a sign-using system, where a system is *conscious* (with respect to signs of a specified kind) when it has both the ability to utilize signs of that kind and the capability to exercise that ability. The ability to utilize signs of a certain kind, of course, is what makes a system a sign-using system (with respect to signs of that kind). The capability to exercise that ability, by contrast, means that the presence of signs of that kind within the appropriate causal proximity would lead—invariably or probabilistically—to an occurrence of cognition. That is the basic conception.

This notion of consciousness has at least three important dimensions. In the first place, it should be distinguished from the concepts of the conscious, the preconscious, and the unconscious advanced by Sigmund Freud (1856–1939), the Austrian founder of psychoanalysis. Even signs that are preconscious or unconscious in Freud's sense might exert an influence upon a semiotic system. In the second place, signs that are too distant to be seen or too faraway to be heard, for example, are signs of which we are ordinarily not conscious by virtue of their causal proximity. In the third place, even signs that are within suitable causal proximity can affect the behavior of a semiotic system only if that system is not incapable of detecting their presence.

When an individual happens to be deaf or blind, blind-folded, or otherwise incapacitated from detecting the presence or absence of signs within a suitable causal proximity, he is incapable of being influenced by them even when they are present. Under ordinary conditions, however, the presence of an external sign tends to create in the mind of a sign user another equivalent or more developed internal sign that stands in the same relationship to that for which it stands as that external sign. When you notice that a red light is lighted at an intersection, your awareness that this is the case creates in you a tendency to apply the brakes, etc., if you want to comply with that sign and come to a complete stop.

More than one sign, of course, can stand for the same thing or have the same meaning. This occurs in the case of icons, indices, and symbols alike. Thus, red lights, octagonal signs, and extended palms (on the arms of policemen) all stand for applying the brakes and coming to a complete halt at an intersection. A low body temperature, an absence of heartbeat, and a lack of brain activity all tend to stand for the cessation of life functions for a human being. But none of these things serves as a sign for a semiotic system unless that system has the ability to utilize signs of that kind either because that ability is acquired by learning or that ability is innate for such a system.

Since the term "concept" is an appropriate term to describe what different signs have in common when they stand for the same thing for a system, let us adopt it here. A complete account of the content of a specific *concept* for a semiotic system (were it possible) would be provided by an inventory of all the kinds of behavior toward which that system would be disposed under all of the different contexts within which it might find itself. The conception of *behavior* required by this approach, however, must be broad enough to encompass mental effects among its possible outcomes, as occurs, for example, when someone attends a lecture and, as a result, "changes his mind."

From this perspective, the theory of meaning presupposes

the theory of action. The theory of action that shall be adopted here takes for granted that *human behavior* and *human actions* are not the same thing. Thus, a person's behavior qualifies as an action when and only when that behavior happens to be brought about (possibly probabilistically) by the causal inter-action of that person's motives, beliefs, ethics, abilities, and capabilities. The success or the failure of our efforts tends to depend upon and vary with the opportunities with which we are presented, as a consequence of whether or not the world is as we take it to be (i.e. as a function of the truth of our beliefs).

A marksman who wants to hit his target (motive) and believes that his target is present (belief) and does not rule out firing at such a target on moral grounds (ethics) can hit his target only if his skills are equal to the task (ability), his rifle and ammunition are available (capability), and the target is within the vicinity (opportunity). When an individual happens to be neurologically impaired, physically restrained, morally debauched, deliberatedly misinformed, etc., then the kind of behavior that he tends to display under otherwise similar conditions varies from those that tend to be displayed by in-dividuals who are not neurologically impaired, physically re-strainted, etc.

The behavior that someone displays on a specific occasion thus results from the complete set of relevant factors present on that occasion, where a factor is relevant when its presence or absence on that occasion made a difference to the strength of the tendency for that individual to display behavior of that kind. The content (or the meaning) of a specific sign (or con-cept) can therefore be captured by identifying its causal role in influencing different kinds of behavior under different kinds of conditions, where those conditions (for human beings) tend to be complex. The same sign thus stands for the same thing for different people, for example, only when they would be disposed to behave the same ways, were they in similar con-texts, when conscious of its presence.

CONNECTIONIST NETWORKS

The theory of mind that has been elaborated here thus appears to have the capacity to contend with the challenge advanced by Fodor that we noted in Chapter 1, namely, that an adequate theory of the mind ought to be able to relate the intensional properties of mental states with their causal capabilities in affecting behavior. From the perspective of the three great problems of the philosophy of mind—the nature of mind, the relation of mind to body, and the existence of other minds—the theory of minds as semiotic systems is (or seems to be) capable of contending with the first and the last (at least, if the capacity to make a mistake—and its variants—are acceptable as criteria).

The principal difficulty that continues to confront this avenue to understanding the nature of mentality and cognition, therefore, is the problem of the relation of mind to body. As it happens, the theory of minds as semiotic systems and the theory of brains as connectionist systems (the most exciting development yet to occur within the domain of cognitive science) appear to complement each other like hand and glove. *Connectionism* views the brain as a neural network of numerous nodes that are capable of activation. These nodes can be connected to other nodes where, depending upon their levels of activation, they may bring about increases or decreases in the levels of activation of those other nodes (Rumelhart et al., 1986; Smolensky, 1988).

Connectionist architectures differ from traditional conceptions in several different ways. One is that connectionist "brains" are capable of parallel processing, which means that more than one stream of data, information, or or knowledge may be processed at the same time. Traditional architectures, such as Universal Turing Machines, for example, only permit single streams of data, information, or knowledge to be processed sequentially rather than simultaneously. Traditional machines can be arranged to process data at the same time, of course, but each such machine remains a sequential processor. Systems, minds, or machines that have the capacity for parallel processing, moreover, certainly ought to possess comparative evolutionary advantages.

Another important difference is the form in which data, information, or knowledge can be stored. In traditional machines, the basic unit of storage is the "bit" (or binary unit), where combinations of bits make up "bytes" (or words). One of the major differences between various kinds of digital machines turns out to be the number of bits that make up bytes for machines of that kind. There are 8-bit, 16-bit, 32-bit, 64-bit . . . word processors, each of which is determined by the physical properties of their machine components. Ultimately, every item of data, information, or knowledge that such a machine can process must be expressible in terms of bits and bytes. In the case of connectionist machines, that role is fulfilled by patterns of activation.

These patterns of activation, in turn, can function as signs for the larger systems of which they are otherwise meaningless parts by coming to stand for other things for the systems of which they are elements. These may include features of their internal states (such as aches and pains of particular kinds) or of their external environments (including objects and properties in the world) as a consequence of the ways these things can function as signs for those systems. Some signs might stand for other things by virtue of relations of resemblance, others by virtue of cause or effect, and still others by virtue of habitual associations. The precise role fulfilled by signs of each of these different kinds, in other words, can be defined by its causal character.

The combinations and permutations of possible neural arrangements is mathematically impressive, indeed. It has been estimated that the number of neurons in the human brain is on the order of 10^{12} (or one trillion) and that the number of connections that each neuron can establish with other neurons is approximately 1,000. This means that there are 10^{15} (or one quadrillion) initial arrangements at any moment in the history of a normal brain, where a "moment" is defined as the least interval of time necessary for such an arrangement to obtain. The potential succession of one arrangement followed by another across time, of course, means that there are enormously more potential sequential states of the mind as a function of 10^{15}!

Suppose, for the sake of illustration, that we took a very small portion of the totality of brain states possible for a specific person, whom we shall call "Rick." The activation of specific neural patterns might stand for specific sounds, while sequences of activation of those patterns might comprise particular melodies. The activation of some specific sequence of patterns would occur whenever Rick heard his piano player play a certain melody in his saloon. It might then turn out that this specific sequence of neural patterns would stand for that melody for Rick and that, when he wanted to hear it once more, he might say to his piano man, "Play it again, Sam!"

Several features of this account merit elaboration. The first, of course, is that the nodes themselves are subsymbolic, which means that they have no inherent meaning as nodes but acquire meaning as elements of arrangements of nodes under appropriate conditions. These conditions themselves would depend upon the kind of semiotic system that a specific system happens to be. Semiotic systems of Type I are more limited in their ability to process information from their environments than are semiotic systems of Type II, and semiotic systems of Type II are more limited in their ability to process information from their environments than are those of Type III.

Second, presumably, neurologically normal human beings, who are all semiotic systems of at least Type III, are subject to similar ranges of sensory stimulation and have similar faculties of learning. This means that they have similar faculties by means of which information from the environment might be processed, but not that they have exactly the same cognitive abilities. Innate genetic differences that affect the speed, the accuracy, and the amount an individual can learn within a fixed interval of time are no doubt present. And physiological differences that affect learning ability—such as the loss of an ear or an eye—would clearly exert their distinctive influence.

Third, the differences between various species could be accommodated within the scope of this approach. For semiotic systems that are subject to classical conditioning, to operant conditioning, to argumentative reasoning, and the like, would tend to fall into a natural scheme of classification which reflects the variety of ways in which they can learn from and be affected by their environments. Yet this approach does not beg the question in assuming that semiotic abilities have to be acquired by means of experience. Quite to the contrary, a dispositional conception does not preclude the possibility that at least some semiotic abilities may be permanent properties of every neurologically normal member of a species. That remains an empirical question.

Indeed, yet another advantage of this approach is that it can accommodate the possibility that human behavior is a probabilistic rather than an invariable effect of its causal conditions. Since the connections that are established between these various subsymbolic neural networks depend not only upon their levels of activation but also upon their predispositions to connect with other elements, it might prove especially promising to entertain these nodes as endowed with probabilistic causal tendencies (or "propensities"). From this point of view, the brain turns out to be a complex arrangement of neural propensities to establish connections under various conditions of system stimulation (that include internal and external stimuli), where different patterns of activation—some of which are meaningful to those within whom they occur—function as causal antecedents of human behavior, including changes in mental states.

BODIES AND MINDS

The interpretation of neurons as endowed with probabilistic causal tendencies holds what may be the key to understanding the connectionist conception. The manner in which states of knowledge, belief, and information are stored in connectionist systems is reflected by the strengths of the tendencies to make connections between various neurons. (Connectionists often refer to these as "weights" instead, but the concept of "strength" is more appropriate within the context of this theory.) Changes in states of knowledge, belief, and information are therefore reflected by changes in the strengths of the tendencies to make connections between these various neurons (from state $S1$ at time $t1$ to state $S2$ at time $t2$). Different strength distributions reflect different states of mind.

The conception of the architecture of the brain as a network of neural propensities, moreover, parallels the conception of the character of a person as a pattern of behavior tendencies. Indeed, insofar as mental propensities parallel behavioral propensities generally, it appears to make a great deal of sense to view the connectionist conception as one that promotes the idea of habits of mind that parallel habits of behavior. Insofar as habits of mind are like habits of behavior, they both invite anaysis from the point of view of dispositions and predispositions. Neural networks thus appear to be predisposed to establish connections between their various neural elements with corresponding strengths of causal tendency under suitable conditions.

The distinctions between bodies and minds now become more evident. The general difference between "brains" and "minds" appears to be exactly what we should have expected all along, namely, that brains are concerned with neurological structures, while minds are concerned with cognitive functions. A special distinction between "brains" and "brain states," on the one hand, and between "minds" and "mind states," on the other, however, also appears to be required in order to reflect the difference between neurological predispositions and dispositions, on the one hand, and between cognitive predispositions and dispositions, on the other. This difference is important.

The introduction of this distinction means that some of our earlier discoveries—especially the definitions that we have employed concerning the nature of minds as semiotic systems—might be ambiguous. The distinction between minds as semiotic systems of Types I, II, III, and so forth requires refinement by distinguishing between semiotic systems as *minds* that are predisposed to become semiotic systems of Types I, II, III, and so forth and semiotic systems as *mind states* that have acquired the ability to exercise mentality of Types I, II, III, and so on. Minds as predispositions and minds as mind states therefore differ in the nature of their cognitive contributions.

Minds as predispositions to acquire mind states, of course, may be predisposed toward their acquisition on the basis of any of the modes of learning, conditioning, and so on that hold for minds of that kind. Minds as semiotic systems of Type I, for example, can be predisposed to acquire the ability to distinguish instances of different colors, shapes, sizes, and so forth on the basis of relations of resemblance. Minds as semiotic systems of Type II might be predisposed to acquire an ability to distinguish instances of different causes or effects (such as smoke and fire) as instances of those causes and effects by means of classical conditioning. And similarly for other kinds of minds.

Brains as predispositions to acquire brain states, of course, may be predisposed toward the acquisition of various specific brain states on the basis of whatever conditions are relevant to bringing about changes in brains and in brain states (which obviously may include surgical procedures as well as other conditions—including individual histories of conditioning—that bring about those changes). What appears to be most important about the brain and its states, however, is that specific cognitive functions (predispositions and dispositions) are related by law to specific neurological structures (predispositions and dispositions). The brain and its states thus seem to be significant because of the light that they can shed upon the mind and its states.

Before turning to the consequences that attend this account for understanding laws of cognition, it may be useful to introduce a figure that represents the kinds of properties that are under consideration here, specifically:

	PREDISPOSITIONS	DISPOSITIONS
OF COGNITIVE FUNCTION	Minds	Mind States
OF NEUROLOGICAL STRUCTURE	Brains	Brain States

Figure 2. Brains and Minds

These distinctions will enable us to identify the basic kinds of relations that may obtain between brains and minds and between brain states and mind states, and thereby clarify the problem of the existence of laws of cognition.

THE LAWS OF COGNITION

Perhaps the first candidates for possible "laws of cognition" that should be considered are laws relating *brains B** as predispositions to acquire brain states to *minds M** as predispositions to acquire mind states. It is plausible to assume that such minds are permanent properties of such brains. Thus, if the permanent-property relation is represented by a subjunctive conditional "... = => ——" when minds are thus related to brains, then the basic form that obtains for laws of this kind (call them laws of cognition of kind 1) would be:

(LC-1) $(z)(t)(B^*zt = => M^*zt)$.

This means that any thing z that were an instance of kind B^* at time t would have to be an instance of kind M^* at that same time. In other words, every thing that happens to be a brain of kind B^* also has to have a mind of kind M^*, because minds of kind M^* are permanent properties of brains of kind B^*.

The truth of laws of form (LC-1) in turn supports the possibility of laws of other kinds. Among their properties, of course, minds of Type III are predisposed to acquire symbolic abilities SA ($SA1$, $SA2$, . . .) falling within some restricted range of possible values (where $SA1$ might be English, $SA2$ might be French, . . .), where its boundaries may be hard to specify. Which of the values (if any) within this range of values happens to be acquired, however, depends upon and varies with environmental—including social and physical—factors EF ($EF1$, $EF2$, . . .) falling within some further range of possible values (where $EF1$ might be having parents who speak English, $EF2$ might be attending an English-speaking grammar school, . . .). Thus, corresponding laws relating minds of kind M^* to the possession of specific semiotic abilities under specific social and physical environmental histories might be formulated, too.

An important difference between laws of cognition of this kind and those of kind 1 is that those of kind 1 reflect properties that things have at a single specific time (as permanent properties) rather than those that come or go as a causal consequence of a process operating across time. Any laws of kind 2 will reflect changes that occur in shifting from an initial mental state $S1$ at a time $t1$ to a later mental state $S2$ at a later time $t2$. Another important difference is that these causal processes that operate across time may be either deterministic or probabilistic, where this difference concerns whether or not exactly the same effect occurs under exactly the same conditions without exception. Such differences have to be reflected by the structure of those laws.

If we employ causal conditionals of universal strength u ("... $=u=>$ ——") and of probabilistic strength p ("... $=p=>$ ——") to represent deterministic and probabilistic causal processes, respectively, laws of cognition of kind 2 can be formulated relating minds M^* to the acquisition of specific symbolic abilities:

(LC-2) (a) $(z)(t)[M^*zt == > (EFzt =u=> SAzt')]$;
 (b) $(z)(t)[M^*zt == > (EFzt =p=> SAzt')]$.

The difference between t and t' represents a specific, fixed interval of time. Thus, laws of cognition of kind 2 (a) represent deterministic causal connections where every mind of kind M^* without exception would acquire semiotic ability of kind SA were it subjected to a history of environmental factors of kind EF. And laws of cognition of kind 2 (b) represent probabilistic causal connections where every mind of kind M^* with probability p would acquire those semiotic abilities were it subjected to a corresponding kind of history.

As we have already discovered, of course, the behavior that arises from the presence of a sign for a human being as a semiotic system is an effect of a complex causal system consisting of specific motives, beliefs, ethics, abilities, capabilities, and opportunities (which tend to depend on the state of the world). Human beings that instantiate some specific fixed set of values for each of these variables are in a complete *mind state* of kind M ($M1$, $M2$, ...) as required. Then corresponding forms of lawlike sentences would assert that subjecting any mind of kind M to a stimulus of kind S would bring about a response of kind R (with either universal or probabilistic strength).

These laws relate specific behavioral responses as effects to their specific stimulus and mind-state causes. They can assume the following forms:

(LC-3) (a) $(z)(t)[Mzt = => (Szt = u => Rzt')]$;
     (b) $(z)(t)[Mzt = => (Szt = p => Rzt')]$.

Thus, laws of cognition of kind 3 (a) represent deterministic causal connections where every mind of kind M without exception would display behavior of kind R were it subjected to a stimulus of kind S. And laws of cognition of kind 3 (b) represent probabilistic causal connections where every mind of kind M with probability p would display that response under those stimuli.

As our discussion of the prospect that we might be nothing but brains in vats was intended to convey, the formulation of these laws as relations that directly relate brains to minds and behavior has to be understood as a simplification, since it omits essential reference to the bodies within which these brains and relations exist. When bodies are damaged, disabled, or in other ways handicapped, that can obviously make an important difference to the outcomes that occur in response to different kinds of environmental factors EF. Strictly speaking, the "$B*zt$"s in (LC-1) and "$M*zt$"s in (LC-2) and so on must be taken as standing for combinations of $B*$-brains/$M*$-minds-in-bodies z at times t and so on, where those bodies have specific features.

Since systems of kind M ($M1, M2, \ldots$) have been characterized with respect to behavioral variables (of motive, belief, ethics, ability, and capability, respectively), it would be appropriate to consider the prospects of discovering some underlying neurophysiological states of kind B ($B1, B2, \ldots$).

These neurophysiological states, of course, are (possibly transient) states of a brain of kind B^*. Nevertheless, states of kind M could be permanent properties of brain states of kind B, in which case laws of yet another kind could be true:

(LC-4) $(z)(t)(Bzt = => Mzt)$.

Any lawlike sentence of this form thus asserts that any system of kind B is—or, better, must be—a system of kind M. Whenever laws of kind (LC-3) and of kind (LC-4) are true, it follows that other laws that assert that subjecting any system of kind B to a stimulus of kind S would tend to bring about a response of kind R (with universal or probabilistic strength) must also be true.

These laws relate specific behavioral responses as effects to their specific stimulus and brain-state causes. They can assume the following forms:

(LC-5) (a) $(z)(t)[Bzt = => (Szt = u => Rzt')]$;
$\quad$ (b) $(z)(t)[Bzt = => (Szt = p => Rzt')]$.

Thus, laws of cognition of kind 5 (a) represent deterministic causal connections where every brain in state B without exception would display behavior of kind R were it subjected to a stimulus of kind S. And laws of cognition of kind 5 (b) represent probabilistic causal connections where every brain in state B with probability p would display that response under those stimuli.

Similarly, when laws of form (LC-1) and laws of form (LC-2) are true, analogous laws of cognition that relate brains of kind B^* and the acquisition of semiotic abilities, for example, must also be true. These laws must have the same forms as those of (LC-2) when the mind variable "M^*" is replaced by the brain variable "B^*" in accordance with laws of form (LC-1) as follows:

(LC-6) (a) $(z)(t)[B^*zt = => (EFzt = u => SAzt')]$;
    (b) $(z)(t)[B^*zt = => (EFzt = p => SAzt')]$.

That z possesses semiotic ability of kind SA, however, does not mean that z also has to be in a mind state M, which consists of specific beliefs, motives, ethics, abilities, and such. The possession of semiotic ability, after all, is a part but is not all of those factors whose presence constitutes a mind state.

This means that semiotic abilities as *features of* mind states need to be differentiated from *mind states* as complete specific fixed sets of values for motives, beliefs, etc. Semiotic abilities SA (the ability to utilize English, for example) are only one aspect of mind states, when they are understood in the broad sense intended here. This reflects the realization that a response to a stimulus tends to occur as an effect of the complete set of relevant factors that affect behavior (including motives, beliefs, ethics, abilities, and capabilities). For the behavior that results from being in a certain mind state is influenced by other factors beyond the ability to use signs alone.

These considerations, I believe, tend to clarify an issue that Chapter 1 left unresolved. It is difficult to contend that brain states are no longer explanatorily relevant in the presence of corresponding mind states, no doubt, when those mind states are permanent properties of those brain states. But we have now discovered an ambiguity implicit in this formulation. A mind state can be a permanent property of a brain state while remaining merely a transient property of the brain of which it happens to be a state. (Go back to the discussion of (LC-4) if this point slipped by!) It therefore follows that sometimes explanations in terms of mind states do have brain-state counterparts, but sometimes not. We shall return to this issue in Chapters 8 and 9.

These paragraphs have been difficult, I know, because most of you are not used to formal modes of thinking, even when they are not *very* formal. Nevertheless, there are excellent reasons for resorting to formulations such as these. The first is that they provide a clear, precise, and economical way to represent large classes of lawlike sentences that possess the same forms. Each of these formulations, after all, implicitly stands for an endless number of specific instances, where each instance fixes the values of their variables. I have no doubt that you can appreciate the advantages that accrue to you from having to understand one kind of law rather than its infinite instances.

The second is that these formulations indicate the kinds of information that are required in order to formulate an adequate explanation for the occurrence of corresponding phenomena. Instances of response behavior of kind R, for example, can be explained by discovering the mind state M relative to which the occurrence of a stimulus of kind S operates as a universal or probabilistic strength cause. Instances of semiotic ability of kind SA can be explained by discovering the M^* minds and the environmental histories EF that brought them about as deterministic or as probabilistic consequences, and so on. They also suggest certain difficulties that can be encountered in formulating scientific explanations by subsuming their instances under laws.

The third, of course, is implicit in the first and the second, but it clearly ought to be emphasized. This discussion of laws of cognition provides very strong evidence that there are laws of this kind. In fact, there appear to be laws of cognition of several different kinds, including laws relating behavior as effect to its stimulus and mind-state causes, laws relating semiotic ability to its mental and environmental causes, and laws relating minds to brains, among other kinds. If there were no laws of cognition, of course, there could be no science of cognition. The prospects for a science of this kind are thus greatly enhanced by the discovery of possible laws appropriate to such an activity.

CHAPTER SEVEN

MENTAL DEVELOPMENT

RATIONALISM AND EMPIRICISM

The conception of brains B^* as connectionist systems of neural nodes of specific kinds, B^*1, B^*2, . . . , no doubt, harmonizes with the possibility that different minds might be endowed with different predispositions to acquire dispositions under different circumstances as a function of the kinds of connections that brains of those different kinds provide. Almost no one, I presume, would want to deny that different species tend to be distinguishable on the basis of the nature of their brains (as "interspecies" differences) and that even different members of the same species can be distinguished on the basis of the nature of their brains (as "intraspecies" differences). Debate on this issue concerns the range in variation that is possible within each species.

This perspective promises to shed new light on an old problem concerning the nature of mind. During the history of philosophy, the school known as *empiricism*, especially as represented by the work of David Hume (1711–1776), an influential Scottish philosopher, has tended to assume that the mind is like a blank slate (or *tabula rasa*) whose content derives from experience. Another school, known as *rationalism*, especially as represented by the work of Immanuel Kant (1724–1804), among the greatest of all philosophers, has suggested instead that the mind is not like a blank slate but rather imposes a certain form upon whatever it can experience. The approach we are pursuing permits us to tackle this issue and to better understand the problem.

Hume was preoccupied with the nature of knowledge, especially with what we can know and how it can be known. He proposed a distinction between two kinds of knowledge, which he referred to as knowledge of "relations between ideas" and knowledge of "matters of fact." Hume maintained that every *idea* worthy of the name (every justifiable, warrantable, or legitimate idea) could be traced back—however indirectly—to some *impression* in experience that gave rise to it. Ideas that cannot meet this standard, however, are unworthy of respect and cannot give rise to any knowledge at all.

This approach may sound vaguely familiar. Indeed, if we think of "impressions" as the vivid and forceful sensations that we experience by means of our five senses of sight, hearing, touch, and so forth, these "impressions" bear a striking resemblance to the notion of observation encountered earlier in Chapter 1. Moreover, if we think of some "ideas" as theoretical and other "ideas" as observable, Hume can be understood to maintain that only ideas that can be reduced to or derived from observations are acceptable. This feature of his approach thus reflects a form of reductionism like that embraced by logical positivism. It ought to be rejected for similar reasons.

The two different kinds of knowledge that are possible for Hume both depend upon the mind's ability to analyze (compare, contrast, combine, etc.) impressions that have arisen in the past. Specific sets of impressions that we have experienced in the past, such as seats with backs and legs, which are suitable for sitting by one person and relatively easily movable, may create in our mind the idea of an object of a certain kind, such as that of a *chair*. For Hume, the idea of a chair consists of a resemblance relation that obtains between that thing's various parts, the regular association of those parts in the form of certain arrangements, and the temporal persistence of specific instances of those arrangements. There is nothing more to this idea.

Nevertheless, ideas like these can give rise to knowledge of two different kinds. The idea of a chair, for example, may enable us to examine the contents of a specific room at one specific time and discover the number of chairs in that room at that time. The belief that, say, there are thirty-six chairs in the room now might be true or might be false, where which it is depends on how many chairs were then in that room. If there were thirty-six, then it is true. This reflects the possibility of knowledge of *matters of fact*. The idea of a chair itself, on the other hand, supports the deduction that, no matter how many chairs are observed at any place at any time, each will be suitable for sitting. This reflects the possibility of knowledge of *relations between ideas*.

Robert Ackermann, a contemporary American philosopher, has noted a subtle tension in Hume's theory of knowledge that emerges at this juncture. Our knowledge of relations between ideas does not seem to possess the kind of uncertainty that affects our knowledge of matters of fact. Our capacity to reason does not appear to be as vulnerable to mistakes as does our capacity for perception. Hume even proposes that mathematical knowledge, such as that represented by algebra and geometry, can be known with certainty. It may be possible to reconcile these elements of Hume's thought, however, as Ackermann suggests, by drawing a distinction between *significant* and *nonsignificant* sentences and adopting the principle that significant sentences (which assert nontrivial claims about experience) are never certain, while certain sentences are never significant (Ackermann, 1965, pp. 182–83).

Even if we are inclined to reject the reductionistic aspect of Hume's position by permitting theoretical ideas that are not reducible to impressions to qualify as potentially significant assertions that might be either true or false (but are not unjustified, unwarranted, or illegitimate on this ground alone), an important core remains. One element of that position is the claim that sentences that are informative about the physical world (by making assertions about the world that are either true or false) cannot be known with deductive certainty. The other element is the claim that sentences that can be known with deductive certainty (by making assertions about ideas that are either true or false) can never be informative about the physical world.

Hume was especially adamant in insisting that knowledge about the future is always uncertain. Inferences about the future on the basis of knowledge about the past, like reasoning from samples to populations or from the observed to the unobserved, depend upon inductive reasoning, which can never be certain. Indeed, Hume was very critical of induction, maintaining that our expectations about the future are mere habits of anticipation that we have acquired on the basis of past experience, but that afford no guarantee that the future will resemble the past. Those expectations cannot be justified, warranted, or legitimated, he believed, because the ideas of causality and lawfulness they implicitly presuppose cannot meet his standard.

While we have already discovered reasons to doubt the suitability of Hume's standard, it was at this juncture that Kant challenged his position. Kant maintained that Hume had erred in mistaking (invariable) modes of functioning of the human mind for mere habits of anticipation. In Kant's view, Hume was partially right (in believing that the specific contents of experience cannot be known apart from experience), but partially wrong (in failing to recognize that the specific forms of experience can be known in advance of experience). Thus, Kant suggested, although we cannot know *what we will experience* in advance of having an experience, we can know *how it will be experienced* relative to these modes of function of the mind. Our challenge in this chapter is to assess the relative merits of these views.

HABITS OF MIND

Kant went much further, moreover, and offered a detailed description of the specific features of experience that the mind imposes on experience in the process of experiencing. These include what he called the "Forms of Intuition" and the "Categories of Understanding." The *Forms of Intuition*, for example, concern the general features of sense experience, with respect to which Kant maintained that, no matter what specific objects we turn out to experience, we will always experience them in terms of Euclidean spatial relations, and that, no matter what specific events we may ever experience, we will always experience them in terms of Newtonian temporal relations.

The *Categories of Understanding*, by comparison, concern the general features possessed by whatever specific objects we happen to experience, with respect to which Kant asserted that, no matter what specific objects we turn out to experience, we will always experience them as substances (or as instances of specific kinds), and that, no matter what specific events we may ever experience, we will always experience them in terms of causal relations (or as having causes and effects). Thus, from this perspective, Kant maintained that Hume was fundamentally mistaken about the nature of knowledge, because some kinds of knowledge about the forms of experience could be possessed in advance of having any particular experiences.

The dispute between Hume and Kant is typically expressed by means of language that Kant introduced but that bears a close correspondence to Hume's own distinctions. Knowledge that can be possessed independently of experience (which does not depend upon experience for its justification, warrant, or legitimacy) is said to be *a priori*, while knowledge that can only be justified, warranted, or legitimated on the basis of experience is said to be *a posteriori*. Sentences whose truth or falsity can be ascertained on the basis of deductive reasoning from our language alone, moreover, are said to be *analytic*, while sentences whose truth or falsity cannot be ascertained on the basis of deductive reasoning from our language alone are said to be *synthetic*. This is not exactly how Kant would have put it, but it is close enough.

From this point of view, the similarities and differences

between their theories of knowledge are easily discerned. Hume maintains that synthetic knowledge is always *a posteriori*, while Kant maintains that some synthetic knowledge is *a priori*. Thus, Kant's position can be diagrammed as follows:

	A Priori Knowledge	*A Posteriori* Knowledge
WITH ANALYTIC CONTENT	Yes	?
WITH SYNTHETIC CONTENT	Yes	Yes

Figure 3. The Rationalist Position

This diagram would reflect the empiricist position instead of the rationalist view if "No" were substituted for "Yes" about synthetic *a priori* knowledge.

Kant's position is fascinating for many reasons, not least of which has to do with the advent of Einstein's special theory of relativity, which relies upon non-Euclidean spatial relations and non-Newtonian temporal relations for understanding the structure of space-time. Euclidean spatial relations assume that, in relation to a point separate from a given line, one and only one line parallel to that line can be drawn, a claim that non-Euclidean geometries (there are two kinds) deny. Newtonian temporal relations similarly assume that, for every event that occurs during the world's history, every other event occurs either before, during, or after that event, which special relativity (with its postulation of the relativity of relations of simultaneity) denies.

A defense of Kant could be devised by emphasizing that, even if it were possible to *think* in terms of non-Euclidean spatial relations and in terms of non-Newtonian temporal relations, it remains impossible to *perceive* whatever we have the capacity to experience within those regions of space-time that are accessible to our senses in non-Euclidean or in non-Newtonian ways. Nonetheless, Hume could protest, first, that the only way we can know how the mind itself functions is on the basis of inductions from experience, and, second, that, no matter how invariably it may have functioned in the past, that provides no guarantee that it will continue to function that way in the future. Even without turning attention to the Categories of Understanding, these points are telling. Is the Kantian position therefore entirely wrong?

Recall that Kant complained that what Hume took to be mere habits of the mind were actually invariable modes of functioning of every (human) mind. The dispositional conception of the mind and the connectionist architecture of the brain both support the importance of the notion of "habits of the mind." Connectionist networks of neural nodes with causal propensities for connecting with other nodes in various arrangements of activation supports the idea of "habits of the brain." Dispositional conceptions of minds as sign-using systems with various strengths of tendency toward behavior of various kinds under specific contextual conditions lend further support to the idea of "habits of behavior." These are three deep and related ideas.

The issues that require further deliberation, I believe, can be phrased in terms of "the habits of the mind." One key aspect of this problem is the extent to which the use of the phrase "*the* mind" itself can be justified, insofar as it implies that there is one and only one kind of mind at stake here. There may be many different kinds of minds, in which case the use of this phrase may require qualification. Notice, in particular, that the existence of other species strongly suggests that there exist different types of minds as predispositions of various kinds of species-specific evolved neural networks.

Another key aspect of this problem is the extent to which the use of the phrase "*the* habits" can be justified as well, insofar as it implies that there is one and only one set of habits at stake here. There may be many different possible habits of mind, even for minds of the same kind (such as particular human minds). It may be that some habits of mind are transient, but that others are not. The search for answers to these questions, therefore, should lead us to consider not only the characteristics, features, or properties that tend to distinguish minds of one kind from those of another but also the circumstances that might justify viewing some "habits of mind" as invariable.

FUNCTIONALLY SIMILAR SYSTEMS

In Chapter 6, a dispositional conception of language and mentality was characterized as a "functionalist conception" because the meaning of primitives is determined by their causal role in affecting behavior. This means that two instances (or "tokens") of specific mental states, such as motives or beliefs, are instances of the same kind (or "type") when and only when they have the same possible causes and possible effects. Since we already know that the actual behavior that a person displays is an effect of the complete set of relevant conditions that he instantiates at that specific time (including his other beliefs, motives, ethics, abilities, and capabilities), we know that this standard must be understood to apply relative to various contexts.

Consider, for example, your belief that you live at a particular address, say, at 2021 East 4th Street in Duluth, Minnesota. This belief has no end of effects under different circumstances. If you discovered that you were lost on a country road and came upon a friendly farmer, you might explain you were from Duluth and ask him for directions. If you discovered you were lost in a seedy section of a major city and ran across a gang of hoods, you might beat a hasty retreat if they asked where you were from. When you want someone to reach you by mail, it helps if you give them your address. If you don't want to hear from them again, you might not mention it at all.

Although your belief is the same, these effects are different, but only because of the influence of context. If a friendly farmer were to offer his help, you would tend to give him the information he needs to be helpful, because you trust him and are in need. If a menacing gang were to come in your direction, you would tend to avoid them if you could, because they could cause you trouble and even harm. Almost all of us would be inclined to behave in the same ways were we to possess the same specific motives, beliefs, ethics, abilities, and capabilities. The proper standard of sameness of meaning is that of similar causes and similar effects in similar contexts.

If we wanted to isolate the specific content of specific tokens, such as the content of a specific belief $B1$, for example, we could do so by holding constant the other beliefs Bm, Bn, . . . , motives $M1$, $M2$, . . . , ethics $E1$, $E2$, . . . , abilities $A1$, $A2$, . . . , capabilities $C1$, $C2$, . . . , and opportunities $O1$, $O2$, . . . , whose presence or absence makes a difference to the (internal or external) behavior that we tend to display in the presence of that belief, $B1$. The content of a specific belief, such as one concerning where we live, thus consists of the totality of tendencies for behavior of different kinds that it would produce in us relative to different contexts. That is what it means.

Whether or not a sign has the same meaning for me and for you, therefore, does not depend upon whether we actually display the same behavior in the presence of that sign. Our actual behavior—the behavior that we do in fact display—would only have to be the same if we happened to find ourselves in the same contexts. (Even then, it would only have to be the same as long as we are not probabilistic causal systems, a point to which we shall return in Chapter 9.) So long as at least some of our motives, beliefs, ethics, abilities, capabilities, or opportunities differ, the behavior that we actually do display does not have to be the same, even when that sign has the same meaning for us both. If that sign does have the same meaning for us both, only the strength of our tendencies to display the same behavior under all and only the same conditions has to be the same—not what we actually do!

From this point of view, there is a crucial difference between ourselves and other human beings, on the one hand, and other animals and machines, on the other. This difference arises from the different kinds of factors that can function as causes or occur as effects of these different kinds of things. The behavior of human beings, after all, can be affected by motives, beliefs, ethics, abilities, capabilities, and opportunities. The behavior of inanimate machines, by comparison, can be affected by other kinds of factors, such as input, software, firmware, hardware, electronic, and magnetic causes in the case of computing machines. The behavior of other animals, of course, falls in between, more like that of human beings and less like that of machines.

Whether different systems properly qualify as having *the same kind of minds* therefore depends upon whether those systems can be affected by the same causes and can produce the same effects. Semiotic systems that can be affected by the same causes and can produce the same effects may be referred to as "functionally similar," while those that cannot may be referred to as "functionally different." Strictly speaking, signs can have the same meaning for different minds only when those minds are minds of the same kind—in other words, only when those minds are functionally similar semiotic systems. Otherwise, those signs cannot be affected by and cannot produce all and only the same causes and effects. How could they?

This means that different human beings tend to qualify as

functionally similar semiotic systems because, as members of the species *Homo sapiens*, they can be affected by the *same* causes and can produce the *same* effects. The relation of functional similarity, however, is obviously amenable to degrees. The animal kingdom abounds with different species, where their degrees of functional similarity depends upon the extent which they can be affected by *similar* causes and can produce *similar* effects. It is relatively easy to think that other members of the primate family, for example, may possess semiotic abilities that differ from us only in degree. But it is hard to imagine that systems that are as functionally different from human beings as Universal Turing Machines could possibly possess similar abilities.

The intriguing question that remains, of course, is whether *any* inanimate machines can have minds. You already know that digital machines do not have minds, because the computational conception of language and mentality is inadequate. The conception of minds as semiotic systems, of course, seems to accommodate the connectionist conception of the architecture of the brain, and conversely. If there can be inanimate connectionist machines—and they are already under construction—then the question becomes not whether they can possess the mental powers of human beings (we know that they can't, since they are functionally such very different kinds of systems), but whether or not they have *any* semiotic ability at all.

EPIGENETIC RULES

Even minds that are of the same kind as functionally similar systems do not have to display all and only the same behavior under all and only the same stimulus conditions. That minds are "functionally similar" only means that they *can* be affected by the same causes and *can* produce the same effects. Whether or not different functionally similar minds actually do have the same strengths of tendencies to display the same behavior under all and only the same conditions depends upon their environmental—including social and physical—histories. The possibility of different minds being in the same mental states does not mean that they ever actually are.

The conception of functionally similar systems as systems that can be affected by the same causes and that can produce the same effects will be instantiated by living things only if they happen to have the same neurological and physiological structures. A free translation of this condition is that functionally similar systems must have the same brains (neurology) and the same bodies (morphology). A technical term for systems with similar bodies and brains is that they instantiate similar "phenotypes." These properties of living things, in turn, arise from specific genetic origins. Another technical term for systems with similar genetic origins (which have similar genes for phenotypes) is that they instantiate similar "genotypes."

Thus, it should be possible, in principle, to relate genotypes to phenotypes to behavior, if we take into account the causal role of mental states. Indeed, to the extent to which our abilities and our capabilities depend on our neurology and our physiology (not to mention the extent to which our minds depend upon our brains), it should be possible to formulate developmental laws that relate genes to bodies to minds to behavior, especially if we take into account the laws of cognition that we discovered in Chapter 6. The systematic study of these relations has been pursued in the past, especially by a community of scholars with a research program investigating the development of different species from the evolutionary point of view.

Charles R. Lumsden and Edward O. Wilson are leading figures in this field, which has come to be known as *sociobiology*. In their books (Lumsden and Wilson, 1981, 1983), they have championed the conception of biological processes that direct or "channel" the development of cognitive processes. The laws that govern them are referred to as *epigenetic rules*.

What is fascinating from the perspective that dominates this book, moreover, is that epigenetic rules turn out to be predispositions for acquiring specific patterns of behavior under the influence of different histories of environmental—including social and physical—factors. Epigenetic rules are dispositional properties of (functionally similar) developing systems.

Different species, of course, are characterized by different epigenetic rules. *Homo sapiens*, for example, has a predisposition toward athletic sports, which may be manifested by acquiring any of a broad range of dispositional abilities to play soccer, tennis, and so forth. Which values within this range of values happens to be instantiated by specific persons depends upon their specific phenotype and their environmental history, including their opportunities for social learning. The ants, by comparison, are completely incapable of acquiring a disposition to play soccer, tennis, and so on, because they lack predispositions toward athletic sports that come with human genes. Perhaps this is why "B.C." comics are so funny!

The approach that Lumsden and Wilson recommend may be illustrated by laws of development of various corresponding kinds. We can rely upon the same formal apparatus as before, starting with causal laws that relate phenotypes to genotypes and to environmental factors, as follows:

(LD-1) (a) $(z)(t)[Gzt ===> (EFzt = u ==> Pzt')]$;
   (b) $(z)(t)[Gzt ===> (EFzt = p ==> Pzt')]$.

As before, the interval from time t to time t' represents a period of time. Laws of development of kind 1 (a) represent deterministic causal connections where every genotype of kind G without exception would acquire a phenotype of kind P were it subjected to a history of environmental kind EF. And laws of development of kind 1 (b) represent probabilistic causal connections where every genotype of kind G with probability

p would acquire a phenotype of kind P were it subjected to a similar kind of history.

We already know that the possession of a phenotype involves possessing a specific neurological type (brain) and a specific morphological type (body). It should come as no surprise, therefore, that every phenotype of kind P will possess a brain of kind B^*, which can be expressed as follows:

(LD-2) $(z)(t)(Pzt ==> B^*zt)$.

It should also come as no surprise that, since every phenotype possesses a brain of a certain kind (in accordance with developmental laws of kind (LD-2)) and every brain of a certain kind possesses a mind of a corresponding kind (in accordance with laws of cognition of kind (LC-1)),

(LD-3) $(z)(t)(Pzt ==> M^*zt)$.

That is, every phenotype of kind P must also possess a mind of kind M^*.

Other developmental laws follow from the laws of cognition that we have previously discovered with the laws of development that we have now encountered. From (LD-2) and (LC-6), for example, we could infer:

(LD-4) (a) $(z)(t)[Pzt ==> (EFzt = u => SAzt')]$;
      (b) $(z)(t)[Pzt ==> (EFzt = p => SAzt')]$.

Laws of these forms assert that every phenotype of kind P would invariably acquire semiotic ability of kind SA were it subjected to environmental factors of kind EF and that every phenotype of kind P with probability p would acquire semiotic ability of kind SA were it subjected to environmental factors of kind EF, respectively. Which form of law might be satisfied by a specific species is a question that empirical research must settle.

Other developmental laws, of course, can be introduced to reflect the influence of histories of environmental factors with respect to the possession of specific brain states and mind states. Presumably, every brain of kind B^* tends to acquire a brain state of kind B as an invariable or probable effect during a history of environmental factors of kind EF as follows:

(LD-5) (a) $(z)(t)[B^*zt = = > (EFzt = u = > Bzt')]$;
   (b) $(z)(t)[B^*zt = = > (EFzt = p = > Bzt')]$.

Moreover, when a mind state of kind M is a permanent property of every brain state of kind B in accordance with (LC-4), it also follows that every brain of kind B^* tends to acquire a mind state of kind M as an invariable or probable effect during a history of environmental factors of that kind:

(LD-6) (a) $(z)(t)[B^*zt = = > (EFzt = u = > Mzt')]$;
   (b) $(z)(t)[B^*zt = = > (EFzt = p = > Mzt')]$.

Other laws follow by combining laws of cognition with developmental laws.

One of the most important benefits that attend the discovery of developmental laws by comparison with laws of cognition is the realization that laws of development of various forms bridge a gap in our laws of cognition. None of those laws directly relate the possession of brains to the possession of brain states (or the possession of minds to the possession of mind states)—except with respect to the acquisition of semiotic ability as a part, but not all, of a mind state in the case of laws of form (LC-2). The reason turns out to be the causal role fulfilled by bodies as well as by brains in the acquisition of brain states and of mind states. There are no laws of cognition that directly relate the acquisition of brain states by brains or of mind states by minds without the mediation of the bodies within which those brains reside.

Consider, for example, the case of laws of form (LC-2), which relate the acquisition of symbolic ability to minds and environmental factors, namely:

(LC-2) (a) $(z)(t)[M^*zt = => (EFzt = u => SAzt')]$;
     (b) $(z)(t)[M^*zt = => (EFzt = p => SAzt')]$.

The possibility that semiotic abilities might be innate (or "instinctive") will be considered in the section that follows. Nevertheless, in general, it would be a mistake to assume that the acquisition of semiotic abilities, in general, could occur without the mediating role of physiology (bodies) that interact with neurology (brains). For laws of form (LC-2) to be true, in other words, the role of physiology must be included among the "relevant factors" *EF* whose presence or absence makes a difference to the truth of such laws.

The acquisition of a language by a human being provides a fascinating illustration of the relations between neurology (brains), physiology (bodies), and semiotic ability (minds). Obviously, no human being has the capacity to learn any language for which he lacks the relevant predispositions. Human languages originate in spoken words. Hence, every language that human beings have developed has to have been constrained by the sounds that human beings can produce. The sounds that humans can produce is determined by their physiology. Indeed, those who work in theoretical linguistics employ the name of *phoneme* to refer to the smallest units of sound to which meaning may be attached that humans can produce by means of their physiology.

The process of acquiring the capacity to use phonemes within a specific class of sounds, moreover, can be viewed as a process of acquiring strengths for connections between neurons. It involves the simultaneous acquisition of habits of brain and of habits of mind. The name *morpheme* is used to refer to the smallest units of meaning that occur within a language, where that language is constrained by the phonemes that are actually employed by the specific communities of language (sign) users under investigation. The morphemes thus reflect the phonemes that have the capacity to affect the behavior of users of that language under suitable conditions of context. Thus, the process of learning human language reflects the interrelations involved in the acquisition of habits of brain, habits of mind, and habits of behavior.

Laws of development of form (LD-4), which make explicit reference to the acquisition of semiotic abilities relative to phenotypes of specific kinds interacting with environmental factors, therefore appear to be more illuminating in this respect than do laws of cognition of form (LC-2). Nevertheless, the discovery of these laws of development that complement the discovery of those laws of cognition ought to be viewed as very strong corroborating evidence that there are laws of both of these kinds. The relations that may obtain between neurology, physiology, and environmental histories for the members of different species are no doubt subtle and complex. But it would be surprising, indeed, were there no laws of these two kinds.

Discovering the forms of these laws is a very different matter than actually discovering the laws themselves, which vary from species to species (with respect to "interspecies" differences) and from individual to individual (with respect to "intraspecies" differences). The specific values of each of these variables—from neurological and physiological structures to kinds of environmental factors to brain states and mind states—has to be discovered through painstaking observations and experiments by neurologists, biologists, zoologists, and the like. Nevertheless, there is something intellectually emancipating about discovering that the existence of laws that relate genes to bodies to minds to behavior is not seriously in doubt. We already know in general what they look like. Our only problem now—the task of science—is to find them.

GENE-CULTURE COEVOLUTION

Lumsden and Wilson (1981) tend to assume that the capacity for social learning is a necessary condition for phenotypes to have "minds." Their identification of "minds" with predispositions to acquire behavior *under the influence of social learning* thus differs from my identification of "minds" as predispositions to instantiate behavior *that involves the utilization of signs*. Their conception of mentality concerns its process of transmission, whereas mine focuses upon its intrinsic semiotic character. If behavior that involves the utilization of signs is sometimes acquired under the influence of social learning, such instances sometimes overlap. But if behavior that involves the utilization of signs ever occurs without the influence of social learning, such instances sometimes diverge. These are distinctive theories of mind.

Perhaps the most important consequence resulting from the choice between these alternatives concerns the prospect for attributing mentality to the lesser species and inanimate machines. The behavioral differences between distinct species, after all, consist in the breadth and variety of those specific ranges of possible behavior that their members can acquire and display as actual dispositions under the influence of (social and physical) environmental factors. The more narrow the range and the less subject to social learning, the greater the justification for regarding that behavior as "instinctual" (as "biologically determined," for animate objects, or as "technologically engineered," for inanimate objects). If semiotic systems are minds—no matter whether they are influenced by social learning—then even "instinctual" behavior by the lesser species (as effects of genetic programs) or by inanimate machines (as effects of computer programs) could still qualify as mental.

If Lumsden and Wilson were right, it would be impossible for instinctual behavior to ever qualify as mental. There are other reasons for thinking that their identification of mentality with social learning is wrong, too. The semiotic approach affords an appealing framework for distinguishing *mental activity* from *nonmental activity* with results that the social learning approach cannot duplicate. Notice, in particular, that many skills (such as the ability to play tennis, soccer, etc.), are acquired under the influence of social learning, yet are not *therefore* obvious examples of "mental activity." As skills involving the acquisition and the utilization of sets of signs, however, playing tennis, soccer, etc., assumes specific dimensions of mentality.

When the members of a species can be influenced by social learning, however, the evolution of that species is no longer dominated exclusively by its genes. Cultural products of previous generations that may have emerged over long periods of time as a consequence of trial and error, conjectures and refutations, and successive approximation can be passed on to successive generations. Patterns of behavior, artifacts of technology, and the like can now become the inheritance of members of a species through a process of cultural transmission, which relieves them of the necessity to rediscover these things for themselves. Successive generations no longer have to "reinvent the wheel" but can build on the discoveries and inventions of their predecessors. And gene-culture coevolution can now occur.

The most fascinating aspect of gene-culture coevolution by contrast to ordinary genetic evolution is that cultures can rapidly evolve, while the pace at which genes can evolve is severely constrained. The rate at which fads and fashions can be transmitted provides an apt example. For these patterns of behavior and products of design can be conveyed to a worldwide population at virtually the speed of light (by means of radio, television, and other modes of mass communication). The rate at which the genes can be transmitted, however, is strongly affected by the period of normal gestation. No matter how intently prospective parents may await the birth of their offspring, it still takes nine months (on the average) to produce a normal baby. Culture can be rushed, but nature takes its time.

Species that can learn from the transmission of culture undoubtedly derive some evolutionary benefits. The survival and reproduction of our species tends to be promoted by medical innovations, including methods of diagnosis (such as X-rays and PET scans) and forms of treatment (such as inoculations against disease and surgical techniques). But species that enjoy these benefits may also run certain subtle risks. The survival and reproduction of our species tends to be threatened by other innovations, including weapons of warfare (such as cruise missiles and atomic bombs) and various by-products of advanced technology (such as automobile exhaust and other forms of pollution). These "benefits" are a mixed bag.

The general conception that emerges from these reflections is that different species are characterized by different neurological and physiological capacities and tendencies. These differences even extend to various stages in the growth and maturation of the members of those species, as Piaget's "Genetic Epistemology," which was discussed in Chapter 1, itself already implies. These changes across time may not only affect our capacity to acquire patterns of behavior but also the strength of our tendencies to display them. The changes that occur between childhood, adolescence, maturity, and old age, after all, influence our inclinations to behave in different ways as well as our ability to learn additional patterns of behavior.

What then can be said on behalf of Kant and Hume? The conclusions that follow suggest that Hume's conception of the mind as a *tabula rasa* cannot be sustained. The bodies and the brains of different species, including man, impose their own distinctive constraints upon the modes of function that they can perform. If the language of thought hypothesis is clearly too strong, Hume's conception of a blank slate is clearly too weak. The Forms of Intuition and the Categories of the Understanding are invariable modes of functioning, however, only if they are permanent properties of every human mind, which is very hard to swallow. It is probably empirically false.

Nevertheless, on the question of the nature of the mind, Kant's views appear to be superior to Hume's. Minds of different kinds *are* functionally different systems. Even minds of the same kind tend to possess the same content only if they have been subject to similar environmental histories. Kant and Hume do not fundamentally disagree on this point. On the question of the nature of our knowledge of the mind, however, Hume's views seem to be superior to Kant's. The only possible way that we can acquire knowledge of the nature of different minds is on the basis of experience.

In suggesting that Kant's conception of the nature of the mind is superior to Hume's, of course, I do not mean to imply thereby that it could not be improved. The distinction between analytic and synthetic sentences requires further elucidation, especially with respect to the crucial role of language. The differences between *a priori* and *a posteriori* knowledge could also benefit from further discussion. These matters will be pursued in Chapter 9. The most important limitation inherent in Kant's thought is that he envisioned the mind as a static rather than as a dynamic structure. The crucial shortcoming of Kant's approach was his inability to fathom the advantages that accrue from the adoption of an evolutionary point of view.

CHAPTER EIGHT

ARE HUMANS RATIONAL?

THE NATURE OF LOGIC

Aristotle (384–322 B.C.), the greatest of all philosophers, was not only a great biologist (the father of biology) but also a great logician (the first formal logician). His theory of classical term logic, for example, endured as an exhaustive account of the subject until the nineteenth century, when a number of revolutionary developments led to the emergence of its modern successors, which are known as sentential logic and as predicate logic, respectively. Indeed, predicate logic is the foundation for almost all research in logic today, where the most important problems involve the introduction of extensions of predicate logic that make it a more powerful and flexible analytic device.

The most basic concept of logic in any of its branches is that of an argument. An argument in this sense need not involve shouting and yelling (or pushing and shoving), even though many arguments in other senses tend to have those features. From the point of view of logic, an *argument* is instead a linguistic entity which consists of a set of sentences divided into two parts, known as "premises" and "conclusion." The conclusion represents a hypothesis, contention, or conjecture that might possibly be true. The premises, by comparison, offer grounds, reasons, or evidence in support of that conclusion. The primary role of logic is to provide standards for evaluating arguments.

As you already are aware, there are two principal branches

of logic, deductive and inductive, and the most significant difference between them is that deductive arguments are intended to be conclusive, but inductive arguments are not. When an argument is conclusive, then its conclusion cannot be false if its premises are true. When an argument is inconclusive, by comparison, its conclusion can still be false even when its premises are true. Neither of these conceptions provides a guarantee that the premises of any argument—deductive or inductive— must be true! That is a question that usually cannot be answered merely by logic alone.

Aristotle's contribution to logic consisted in providing a complete set of rules and procedures for assessing the properties of arguments constructed of sentences having special forms. These sentences were restricted to four forms, which are known as "A," "E," "I," and "O" sentences. They are of the forms, "All Xs are Ys," "All Xs are non-Ys," "Some Xs are Ys," and "Some Xs are non-Ys," respectively. The "Xs" and the "Ys" are place holders for names or descriptions of specific things or kinds of things, where these expressions in turn are known as "terms." Sentences of these four kinds are called "categorical sentences" and are governed by what is called *classical term logic*.

Aristotle was especially concerned with two kinds of arguments, those that consist of one premise and one conclusion (which he called *immediate inference*) and those that consist of two premises and one conclusion (which he called *syllogistic inference*). Subsequently, we shall distinguish arguments from inferences, but here his terminology should stand. Aristotle's system of classical term logic was therefore devoted to a systematic identification of all the kinds of immediate inference and of syllogistic inference that actually are conclusive, where such arguments are said to be "valid." For valid arguments, their conclusions cannot be false, so long as their premises are true.

One of the most important distinctions that can be drawn

in logic thus arises at this juncture. While arguments may be said to be "valid" in virtue of their form, they are said to be "sound" in virtue of their content. Somewhat more precisely, the validity of an argument can guarantee the truth of its conclusion only on the condition that its premises are true. What makes an argument "sound" is that it is both valid and has true premises. Thus, no special genius is required to generate valid arguments. "If you are the president, then your wife is the first lady; you are the president; therefore, your wife is the first lady" is a valid argument, even when you are not married.

Aristotle displayed considerable ingenuity in the invention of ways to say whatever could be said by means of categorical sentences. A sentence about a specific individual, such as "Socrates is mortal," for example, is not a sentence that appears to satisfy any of the four categorical forms. But, in Aristotle's view, it could be expressed as an "A" sentence when its meaning was subject to paraphrase. For surely things-that-are-identical-with-Socrates must be Socrates, in which case the sentence "Socrates is mortal," could be rendered, "All things-that-are-identical-with-Socrates are things-that-are-mortal." Other problematic sentences might receive similar treatment.

For more than two thousand years, classical term logic was supposed to exhaust the scope of deductive logic. Gottlob Frege (1848–1925), however, destroyed this illusion by introducing the conception of the *sentential function*, an expression that could be turned into a sentence of one or another different kind through different logical operations. This idea became the foundation for modern predicate logic, relative to which classical term logic should be viewed as a special case. Since the nineteenth century, deductive logic has made enormous strides forward, which have extended the scope of logic far beyond the forms of argument expressible by means of categorical sentences alone.

It may be tempting to imagine that deductive arguments are the only kind we need, but that would be false. Any time that we draw an inference from the past to the future, from the observed to the unobserved, or from a sample to a population, we employ inductive logic. This field is not as well developed as is deductive logic, but similar distinctions have to be drawn. An inductive argument that has an appropriate form, for example, may be said to be "proper," while an argument that is both proper and also has true premises may be said to be "correct." Strictly speaking, therefore, deductive logic studies valid argument forms while inductive logic studies proper ones. Reasoning of both kinds appears to be essential to our survival as a species.

HUMAN RATIONALITY

In order to appreciate the evaluative function of logic, it is important to realize that there is a fundamental difference between the source of an idea (its origin, where it came from) and the value of an idea (its truth, why it is important). We encountered this distinction in Chapter 4, where the context of discovery and the context of justification were introduced. What is most important about logic in relation to this distinction is that logic applies within the context of justification rather than within the context of discovery. I admit that there are those who would dispute this contention by arguing in favor of a "logic of discovery," but this distinction is still a fundamental one.

In reflecting upon the nature of logic, therefore, it is crucial to distinguish between the process of thinking and the products of thought. When we are trying to come up with ideas (a subject for a term paper, a proposal for a school project, etc.), it would be silly to imagine that we should have to satisfy the conditions for validity or for propriety. In coming up with ideas, it is ordinarily not important where they came from. But it is important how well they withstand critical scrutiny. Even famous figures in the history of science, such as Johannes Kepler and even Sir Isaac Newton, may have been inspired by unscientific ideas in the course of making scientific discoveries.

A detective investigating a case, for example, might spend time lost in thought about a specific suspect and think that he may have committed the crime. What becomes important in the eyes of the law is not whether such a hunch emerged from a daydream but whether it can be supported by the evidence. For criminal cases, the standard tends to be proof "beyond a reasonable doubt" as determined by a jury evaluating the evidence according to legal procedure. Even laws of society, in other words, take account of the difference between the context of discovery and the context of justification.

How well a jury may perform in carrying out its responsibilities before the law, no doubt, tends to be influenced by many different factors, including the extent to which its members are open to the influence of evidence. No one can receive a fair trial if the jury has a closed mind or is unwilling to consider what both sides have to say. In this respect, the members of the jury are supposed to be amenable to rational persuasion, which means that the findings at which they arrive are supposed to be supported by grounds, reasons, or evidence that has been introduced during the course of the trial.

When a jury is rational, presumably its reasoning is governed by principles of logic. One of the most elementary principles of inductive logic, however, is known as *the requirement of total evidence*. This condition does not mean that the members of a jury have to know everything there is to know about a case in order to arrive at any decision. Only God could possibly know all there is to know about these things. What it means is that a responsible decision should be based upon all of the evidence that is both available and relevant, where previous investigations and legal procedures have led up to presentations in the courtroom by the defense and by the prosecution.

It is fascinating to realize that it is up to the jury to put things together in accordance with the requirement of total evidence. The defense counsel, for example, may be expected to plead his side of the case, which means he will tend to offer evidence that exonerates his client. The prosecution, by contrast, will tend to offer evidence that incriminates the accused. Neither of these officers of the court is expected to satisfy the canons of inductive reasoning, precisely because their roles are predefined. Each offers what he believes is most persuasive to supporting his side of the case, leaving it to others to sort things out. The jury has to weigh the evidence for itself.

If human beings were not amenable to rational persuasion, of course, trial by jury would be pointless. Whether or not human beings can be rational, therefore, appears to be a significant question of principle to which courtroom practice suggests an affirmative answer. A necessary condition would seem to be that rationality must be inherited or be acquired. If rationality can be inherited genetically or acquired culturally, however, then human beings must have the capacity to be rational. Depending on the nature of rationality, it might be a permanent or a transient human property. Indeed, rationality might even be a highly specialized ability rather than a more general capacity or ability. Perhaps there is no such thing as an IQ. Or perhaps there are IQs for names and faces, IQs for mathematics, etc.

A variety of views on this subject are possible. Aristotle himself was inclined to think that this capacity was distinctive to human beings. Thus, he distinguished between *plants* (capable of generation and reproduction), *animals* (capable of voluntary movement and feeling sensations in addition to generation and reproduction), and *men* (capable of rational persuasion in addition to voluntary movement and feeling sensations in addition to generation and reproduction). As almost everyone knows, Aristotle thereby defined man as the rational animal. His definition, moreover, was intended to be restricted to male citizens. He was less sanguine about women and slaves.

We can readily improve upon Aristotle's definition, therefore, by embracing the conception of *human beings* as rational animals. This view is heartening, insofar as it suggests that human beings are at least semiotic systems of Type IV. Nevertheless, a number of problems seem to attend this view. One is that the idea of rationality itself appears to stand in need of further elaboration. There may be at least three distinct conceptions of rationality that deserve to be distinguished. Moreover, if rationality is a property of human beings, is it permanent or merely transient? Is this a property that no human being could be without? Can rationality evolve? These are the questions we shall pursue in this chapter and the next one.

RATIONALITY OF ACTION

The idea of human rationality is an extremely broad one, encompassing both action and belief. The notion of *rationality of belief* concerns the extent to which humans tend to accept and to reject beliefs more or less in accordance with the evidence at their disposal. The notion of *rationality of action*, by contrast, concerns the extent to which humans tend to act in accordance with their beliefs and motives to attain their desired ends. There is even a notion of *rationality of ends*, insofar as the ends human beings desire can also be more or less rational. Indeed, since rationality of ends will be the least familiar of these notions, perhaps it should be considered first.

As a rule, ends are rational only when they are not impossible to attain. The accent is on the word "impossible." If someone wanted to prove that 4 is an odd number, for example, that would be an irrational thing to want to do, because it is logically impossible. Or if someone wanted to travel faster than the speed of light, that would be an irrational thing to want to do, because it is physically impossible. Or if someone with an older sister wanted to be the firstborn in his family, that would be an irrational thing to want to do, because it is historically impossible. Such ends are irrational because their attainment would involve violating laws of logic, of nature, or history.

There is nothing wrong with attempting things that are improbable or difficult or merely hard, of course. And sometimes things like this are said to be "impossible." (Before you were admitted, for example, you may have thought that it would be impossible for you to go to college.) What makes an end "impossible," by comparison, is that it is literally rather than merely figuratively impossible. These are things that cannot be done. Naturally, I would admit that sometimes we may believe something is impossible when it actually is possible. If the special theory of relativity were to turn out to be false, traveling faster than the speed of light might be possible, after all.

Our judgments about what is and is not logically, physically, and historically impossible, therefore, are relative to our *beliefs* about what is and is not logically, physically, and historically impossible. These are issues about which we might be wrong. Whether something is or is not impossible or is or is not an irrational end, therefore, is something about which we may not always be entirely certain. These judgments merely reflect our understanding concerning the laws of logic, the laws of nature, and the world's history. When our understanding of the laws of logic, the laws of nature, or the history of the world are at fault, we can clearly arrive at mistaken judgments.

If rationality of ends is relative to the laws of logic, the laws of nature, and the history of the world, then rationality of action is relative to our motives, our beliefs, our ethics, our abilities, our capabilities, and our opportunities. When we want to secure an end and the appropriate means are at hand, when they are not ruled out on moral grounds and we have an ability to utilize them we are not incapable of exercising, then acting on those motives, beliefs, ethics, abilities, and capabilities exemplifies rationality of action. The success of our actions cannot be guaranteed (since some of our beliefs could be false and the opportunity only an illusion), but they can still be rational.

Perhaps the principal difficulty we confront in explaining one another's behavior concerns the problem of access to the kinds of information that we would need to have in order to be able to do so. We often do not know why others act as they do because we are ignorant or unaware of the specific motives and beliefs that brought their behavior about. The fascination that we find in learning about the bizarre or the fantastic behavior that others display no doubt derives largely from the sense of discovery that the reasons they acted as they did were reasons that, often as not, were we in their situation, we could easily understand. But that is not always so.

Suppose that a young woman discovered someone had entered her apartment during the middle of the night. Surely knowing only that we could not explain or predict her behavior; there are simply too many missing factors. Suppose, for example, that she immediately recognized her boyfriend to whom she had given a key. In that case, we would not expect her to yell for help or to defend herself from his approach. Suppose, however, that she gradually realized that this person had been following her during the day, that his manner was extremely menacing, and that she might be subject to rape. In that case, we expect her to yell and to defend herself from his approach.

Admittedly, there is always room for argument about specific cases, especially since other factors may make a relevant difference. Had there been a series of sexual attacks in the neighborhood where those who resisted had been harmed, while those who had not resisted had not been harmed, then were this something of which she were aware, it might have made a difference to her behavior. The rationality or irrationality of an action is always a matter of degree, where the behavior displayed is more or less in accord with the motives, beliefs, ethics, etc., that brought it about. But success in measuring that degree of rationality can be a difficult and complex matter.

Nevertheless, there are cases in which irrationality appears to be the only explanation for the phenomenon at hand. Consider, for example, the experimental observations of Amos Tversky, a well-known psychologist at Stanford University. Tversky has discovered that the manner in which an option is described can make a difference to the behavior of an individual, even in cases in which it presumably should not. These are cases in which the same situation is described in two different ways (such as a glass that is said on one occasion to be "half empty," on another occasion to be "half full") where these different descriptions would be thought to be irrelevant.

An example of Tversky's findings might be something like the following. An individual who is supposed to have cancer is told that patients who receive treatments of kind T have an eighty percent survival rate. Alternatively, the same individual is told that patients who receive treatments of kind T have a twenty percent mortality rate. By a ratio of about two to one, subjects prefer the eighty percent survival option over the twenty percent mortality option. Since any option with an eighty percent survival rate also has a twenty percent mortality rate and any option with a twenty percent mortality rate also has an eighty percent survival rate, these are merely two different descriptions of one and the same choice. They ought to be equally preferable.

The discovery that these alternatives are not viewed as comparable or the same strongly suggests that these decisions are not completely rational. Other situations indicate that irrationality of action is not the exclusive province of the subjects of psychological experiments. Most of us have discovered that it is easier to commit ourselves to a diet than it is to stay on one. If we find ourselves eating more and exercising less, while maintaining we are serious about losing weight, then we are either kidding ourselves in order to feel better or sincerely misdescribing the situation to others or displaying a modicum of irrationality of action. Which is which I leave for you to decide.

RATIONALITY OF BELIEF

There are several facets to rationality of belief, only some of which are related to questions about reasoning. Our beliefs about the world, after all, can receive evidential support from our perceptual inferences as well as on the basis of deductive or inductive inference. The term "inference" should be used whenever we want to refer to mental processes of reasoning rather than to those linguistic entities known as "arguments." Thus, deductive and inductive inferences are mental activities involved in deriving new beliefs from old beliefs, for example, where the old beliefs stand as premises to the new beliefs as conclusions. Both presuppose the availability of "premises."

The principal difference between perceptual inference and these other modes of inference, therefore, is that perceptual inferences do not presume the existence of grounds, reasons, or evidence in the form of premises from which other conclusions may be drawn. Indeed, perception merely involves describing the contents of experience by means of language. It presupposes only the ability to use signs of certain kinds and the capacity to exercise that ability in the presence of those signs. The extent to which anyone can use a language to accurately describe the world around them, however, obviously depends upon their own physical condition and their understanding of language. Those who are blind, color-blind, etc., may not perform especially well.

The causal influence of illusions, delusions, and hallucinations, of course, can be very great. You may want to avoid driving into the large lake that looms before you as you cross the desert. It may even be difficult to bring yourself to realize that it is simply a mirage. More than a few human beings have done harm to themselves and others because of sights and sounds that others viewed as flights of fantasy. The problem thus becomes establishing some standard for assessing when perceptual inferences fall within a range of acceptability and when they fail to do so. This is not a completely trivial matter, since unacceptable perceptual inferences can lead to the funny farm.

The use of standardized tests for vision and for hearing, no doubt, provides procedures that benefit the community, from this point of view. More interesting to contemplate, therefore, is the extent to which deviations from appropriate standards of deductive and inductive inference actually occur. Most of us are fairly proficient at deriving obvious conclusions from obvious premises, once we think about them. We usually succeed in obeying simple rules of logic, including *modus ponens* (given *if p then q* and *p*, infer *q*) and *modus tollens* (given *if p then q* and *not-q*, infer *not-p*), for example.

But most of us are not especially adept at deriving subtle conclusions from complex premises, even when we want to think them through. And in the case of inductive reasoning, the situation is even more complicated, because the proper principles of inductive inference are matters of debate. (See, for example, Michalos, 1969, Part II.) Whether or not human beings exhibit rationality of belief, of course, becomes extremely difficult to measure in the absence of agreed-upon standards of inductive inference. For the sake of illustration, I shall mention one conception that has been explored in recent work on subjects such as these, namely, the *availability hypothesis*. (It is discussed, for example, by Cosmides, 1985, pp. 77–82.)

The availability hypothesis maintains that the strengths of associative links that have been established during the subject's personal experiences are directly proportional to the number of exposures that that person has had to each such pairing. The strength of the association that relates the content described by *p* and the content described by *q* is proportional to the relative frequency with which q-content has occurred in relation to p-content during that person's life. If p-content has occurred n times and q-content has occurred m times in relation to p-content, then the strength of association r for that person linking q with p should be equal to $m/n = r$.

This sounds more complicated than it should. Suppose, for example, that you had been to six Harrison Ford movies and throughly enjoyed five of them (perhaps *Blade Runner* didn't appeal to you). In that case, the strength of association with which you would associate positive feelings with Harrison Ford movies would be five-sixths. Suppose, for another, that you frequently dine at a local restaurant called "Porter's." You may have had a specific meal, say, Veal Oscar, on n occasions and liked the meal on m such occasions. In that case, the strength of your association of liking the meal in relation to ordering Veal Oscar at Porter's would have the value $r = m/n$.

This hypothesis represents a psychological and personalized version of what is often referred to as as the *straight rule* of induction. According to the straight rule, if m/n observed As have been Bs, infer that m/n As are Bs. It can be contrasted with other inductive rules, such as the *counterinductive rule*, according to which, if m/n observed As have been Bs, infer that $1 - m/n$ As are Bs, and the *a priori rule*, according to which, if m/n As have been observed to be Bs, infer that k As are Bs (where k is an arbitrary constant). The first rule treats the available evidence as though it were always representative, the second as though it were always inversely representative, and the third as though it were always irrelevant (Salmon, 1967).

Thus, to extend our examples, the counterinductive rule would have it that if you had enjoyed five-sixths of the Harrison Ford movies you had seen in the past, then your strength of association should now be merely one-sixth (as a matter of counterinduction). The *a priori* rule, by contrast, would have it that if you decided that you liked Veal Oscar then no matter how often you were disappointed with such a meal at Porter's, you should always order it anyway (as an *a priori* policy). These last two inductive rules may not be serious candidates for proper reasoning, but still others—such as reliance upon Bayes' Theorem and "inference to the best explanation"—surely are.

In view of these complications, it should come as some relief that psychological experiments suggest that human beings are reasonably competent, at least with respect to deductive reasoning. Peter Wason and Philip Johnson-Laird, for example, have reported that recent experiments testing children's reasoning with *modus ponens* and with *modus tollens* (which appear to me to have been properly conducted) exhibited a remarkable capacity for valid inference, even among six- and eight-year-olds. A child, for example, is asked, "If that boy is John's brother, then he is ten years old. That boy is not ten years old. Is he John's brother?" (Wason and Johnson-Laird, 1972, p. 41). The responses of these subjects were usually correct.

EVOLUTION AND RATIONALITY

We still have to ask if evolution is compatible with rationality. A significant debate concerning human behavior and its evolution has recently emerged between two important and influential groups of scholars. One of these groups represents the research program of "Darwinian anthropology," the other the research program of "evolutionary psychology." The key issue that divides them is the extent to which the human mind should be viewed as a single unified general-purpose reasoning processor or as a modular assembly of special-purpose psychological mechanisms. If this sounds rather familiar, it should, because a similar difference separated Hume from Kant.

The difficulties that confront attempts to establish empirical evidence that might discriminate between these hypotheses are substantial. One of the more important of these research programs extends from studies in the psychology of reasoning by Wason and Johnson-Laird to the advocacy of so-called "Darwinian algorithms" by Leda Cosmides and John Tooby. The support they find for evolutionary psychology may or may not justify the view that human reasoning is governed by domain-specific psychological mechanisms, because the arguments that they offer are difficult to assess. (For an introduction to these issues, see Cosmides, 1985 and Davies et al., 1995.)

The significance of their findings, as you might expect, depends upon the specific variety of "logical reasoning" under consideration. There seem to be several features of Cosmides' research, in particular, that raise some troublesome problems. Tests of reasoning involving material conditionals, for example, may not be appropriate for representing ordinary thinking, especially when it concerns causal processes using causal conditionals instead. Tests that focus exclusively upon deductive reasoning, for another, may misinterpret findings involving the use of inductive reasoning, which appears to have a central role to fulfill with respect to human evolution.

Indeed, principles of reasoning such as *modus ponens* and *modus tollens* represent the kind of domain-general reasoning capacities that ought to be entertained as a proper alternative to the Darwinian algorithm hypothesis. In application to causal conditionals, for example, they are content independent across such domains as physics, chemistry, biology, and so on. Their successful use presupposes the possession of a considerable amount of domain-specific knowledge, of course, because their truth hinges on the presence or absence of every relevant property. But that is another thing.

Since six- and eight-year-old children display considerable capacity for logical reasoning, the question of whether evolution is compatible with rationality deserves an affirmative answer. Whether rationality in the sense of a capacity for logical reasoning should be regarded as inherited or as acquired, however, has not yet been settled. But it should be evident by now that the human species possesses either a genetic predisposition to acquire the ability to reason logically under certain very general conditions or else a disposition to reason logically that tends to be displayed except under rather unusual conditions. This issue is pursued in Chapter 9.

The issue raised by the debate between the evolutionary psychologists and the Darwinian anthropologists, I believe, may turn out to be the same as that between Kant and Hume. Indeed, it may bear marked similarity to the difference between connectionist and ordinary digital machines. If the key element of the positions of evolutionary psychology, Kant, and connectionist machines turns out to be the existence of natural laws relating brain states to mind states, such as laws of form (LC-4), introduced in Chapter 6, then the key aspect of the positions of Darwinian anthropology, Hume, and ordinary digital machines may be the possibility that the same brain state B can be related to different mind states $M1, M2, \ldots$, on various occasions.

Such a prospect may be well-founded in the case of digital machines, which lack the semiotic ability that would enable them to attach semantic meaning to the syntactic strings that they process. What those mean can clearly differ from one user to another. In the case of general-purpose (or *tabula rasa*) systems, however, things are far less clear. On the assumption that they can be semiotic, it is difficult to imagine how different mind states $M1, M2, \ldots$, could attend the same brain state B for such systems. Perhaps this might be both true (but trivial) for digital machines and significant (but false) for semiotic systems—and consequently it seems more intriguing than it should!

CHAPTER NINE

MENTALITY, CAUSALITY, MORALITY

COMMUNICATION AND CONVENTION

The conjecture that humans possess domain-specific reasoning modules, on its face, is no more and no less plausible than the conjecture that humans possess domain-specific sensory modalities. Since humans possess domain-specific sensory modalities (for vision, hearing, and smell, for example), that conjecture should not be dismissed out of hand. Indeed, there is a considerable body of neurological and physiological evidence that different cognitive functions tend to be carried out within different parts of the brain. (See, for example, Edelman, 1987.) The results of Chapter 8, therefore, should not be interpreted as suggesting that humans have no evolved psychological mechanisms for performing cognitive functions. The opposite is far more likely.

This question has at least two aspects. One concerns whether a specific cognitive function (such as a special kind of semiotic ability) may have become a part of the genetic program for every member of a certain species. If Fodor's language of thought hypothesis were true, for example, then the language of thought ("mentalese") would be an innate (or "instinctive") trait of every (neurologically normal) human being. All (neurologically normal) human beings would have to possess the same language of thought, no matter what environmental history they happened to endure. In this case, an evolved psychological mechanism for this cognitive function would exist.

The other concerns the specificity of cognitive function that such an evolved psychological mechanism should possess. One of the most implausible features of Fodor's account appears to be the rich and extensive set of psychological primitives that is presupposed. In order for mentalese to be equal to the task of providing primitives by means of which any predicate in any ordinary language might be understood, it has to have enormous resources (sufficient, for example, to accommodate any scientific discovery or technological innovation *before it has occurred*). The hypothesis of evolved psychological mechanisms in the form of predispositions for acquiring ordinary languages within some specific range of possible languages under suitable environmental conditions is surely a far more plausible conjecture (Fetzer 1992).

A pragmatical conception of language and mentality generates reasonable conceptions of consciousness and cognition, as Chapter 6 has explained. *Consciousness* combines the ability to use signs with the capability to detect them when they are present within suitable causal proximity of a sign user. *Cognition* occurs when a sign of a certain kind occurs within a suitable causal proximity of a system that has the ability to use signs of that kind and is not inhibited in the exercise of its ability from detecting that sign's presence. While consciousness combines ability and capability, cognition combines consciousness with opportunity. But a pragmatic account also helps us to understand the circumstances that can bring about (un)-successful *communication*.

It should be evident that when a speaker $z1$ utters a sentence (uses an icon, employs a symbol, etc.), successful communication with a hearer $z2$ will generally take place only to the extent to which both speaker and hearer interpret that sentence in similar ways. This can be a matter of degree. When $z1$ and $z2$ would have the same strengths of tendencies across every set of relevant conditions when conscious of that sign (when their contexts were the same for both), then that sign possesses the same meaning for $z1$ and for $z2$ even when their actual behavior differs (either because their contexts are not the same or because their dispositions are probabilistic). If they would have behaved in similar/somewhat similar/ . . . ways, then it possesses similar/somewhat similar/ . . . meaning for both; and so forth.

When the same sign means more than one thing to different users of the same system of signs, then that sign is ambiguous. The exact proportion of a specific population for which the same sign means one thing rather than another, however, cannot be ascertained *a priori*. Even though the fundamental determinant of meaning for the individual is by means of *specific habits* (or "habituation"), the fundamental determinant of meaning for the community is by means of *the same* specific habits (or "convention"). The principal method for promulgating the same specific habits within the community, of course, turns out to be by forms of education and training in the customs, traditions, and practices that are distinctive of that community.

There thus appear to be at least three different ways in which specific skills and other cognitive functions could be possessed by the members of a community. The first is by *nature* as a causal consequence of possessing a specific genotype, where the same skills and cognitive functions must be possessed by all members of that species independently of their specific environmental histories. The second is by *habituation* as a causal consequence of acquiring specific habits, skills, or dispositions, where the possession of those skills and cognitive functions is an effect that arises from the causal interaction of specific predispositions and specific environmental histories.

The third is by *convention* as a causal consequence of the influence of specific predispositions and specific environmental histories, where those histories include the influence of customs, traditions, and practices, transmitted by means of education and training within those communities. The crucial difference between nature, on the one hand, and habits and conventions, on the other, no doubt, is that properties that we have by nature are permanent properties no normal member of that species could be without. Different members of the same species are capable of possessing different habits or of adopting different conventions only if they are not "by nature."

The crucial difference between habituation, on the one hand, and convention, on the other, is that, even though both reflect transient properties that normal members of the species could be without, the effects of conventions are intended to promote a degree of uniformity in the habits of a community. The principal benefits of possessing a certain degree of uniformity in the habits of a community, moreover, appear to be twofold in strengthening the prospects for successful communication between its members and in thereby enhancing opportunities for successful cooperation between them. Ultimately, the propriety of viewing a collection of individuals as a community depends upon its members' potential for communication and cooperation.

From this point of view, the acquisition of a common language seems to provide an essential ingredient in the development of a human community. The results that have been discovered here suggest that conventions function as social mechanisms for resolving differences and for codifying practices concerning what does and does not qualify as "standard practice" within particular language-using communities. While conventions are secondary to habituation in relation to the acquisition of a language, the acquisition of common forms of habituation that facilitate communication and cooperation between their members appears to be indispensable to the emergence of human communities. Without common language, no true community can exist.

TRANSIENT RATIONALITY

In his reflections on the character of human rationality, Philip Johnson-Laird (1983) has noticed three distinct points of view.

Some theoreticians, especially philosophers, tend to assume that humans are invariably rational. Other theoreticians, especially psychologists, tend to assume that humans are invariably irrational. Nevertheless, he suggests, there is yet another, third, alternative, namely, that thinking may be a skill, the performance of which may vary with expertise. In this case, humans might be rational in some circumstances, but not rational in others. The theses of invariable rationality and of invariable irrationality therefore have to compete with the thesis of variable rationality, for which considerable evidence can be found.

Strictly speaking, it is important to differentiate between rationality or irrationality, on the one hand, and nonrationality, on the other. A person can be *irrational* only with respect to some dimension (action or belief, for example) with respect to which he can tend to be *rational*. Whether or not we are hungry when we arise in the morning is not a matter of rationality at all. It would make no sense to describe *hunger* as a rational or as an irrational state. Being hungry is no more rational or irrational than is being six feet tall, unless, for example, that state of hunger were a psychosomatic symptom of some abnormal condition. Then it might be irrational, after all.

The choice of one means rather than another to attain a certain goal under specific circumstances or the adoption of one belief rather than another in the possession of specific evidence, however, may be more or less rational actions or beliefs. As I observed in Chapter 8, rationality of action has to be distinguished from rationality of belief. Indeed, there is a scale (or "continuum") of grades (or "degrees") of rationality and irrationality of action or of belief, when these notions are adequately understood. Different persons might be high in rationality of belief but low in rationality of action, or high in rationality of action but low in rationality of belief. It is not necessary to be high in both or to be low in both. All of these combinations are possible.

The theses that Johnson-Laird ascribes to philosophers and to psychologists, of course, would be explainable were rationality or irrationality, respectively, permanent properties of every (neurologically normal) human mind. From this perspective, the principal difference between the hypothesis of thinking as a skill and those of invariable rationality or irrationality is that only the hypothesis of thinking as a skill envisions "rationality" as a transient property that different members of the same species may or may not share. Their differences in these respects might then be explainable as effects caused by particular environmental conditions, which would reflect differences between them with respect to education, training, and culture.

The position that Johnson-Laird presents concerning human rationality harmonizes with the consequences we have discovered concerning natural language. This should not be especially surprising, given the close connection between the use of language and the nature of thought that has been explored thoughout this book. Nevertheless, some of the consequences attending these findings might be unexpected. The implications that follow include, for example, (1) that different individuals may vary enormously with respect to the extent to which they are rational (in any of its senses), and (2) that explanations for any particular individual's behavior should not be based upon any general assumptions (or "postulates") of rationality.

The extent to which different individuals display rationality of action and rationality of belief appears to depend upon the extent to which their habits of behavior and their habits of mind are those most appropriate to their objective, aim, or goal. Individuals exemplify rationality of belief to a high degree, for example, when there is a high degree of correspondence between the patterns of thought that they instantiate as habits of mind and suitable standards of inductive and deductive reasoning. It is often assumed that students of logic are more likely to exemplify rational patterns of thought than are those who have never studied formal subjects. Those who have never studied logic, however, may still be very logical in their reasoning, just as others who have studied logic (alas!) may still be quite illogical.

Other consequences that follow concern our understanding of ordinary language. Notice, for example, (3) that various individuals may greatly differ in relation to the extent to which they speak the same language (in any of its senses), and (4) that explanations for an individual's behavior should not be based upon any general assumption (or "postulate") that contradicts this realization. Individuals can use the same (or different) grammar and rely upon the same (or different) vocabulary and yet mean the very same (or very different) things. Ultimately, the only suitable measure of the degree to which different individuals mean the same thing by the words and other signs that they employ is that the strength of their tendencies to behave one way rather than another would be similar in the same contexts.

The precise meaning which different individuals attach to otherwise similar signs, therefore, can be very difficult to ascertain. From the point of view of methodology, this conception displays what Hempel (1962) has called "the epistemic interdependence of motive and belief attributions" or—better—the epistemic interdependence of motive, belief, ethics, ability, capability, and opportunity attributions. This means that, to subject hypotheses of any of these various kinds to an empirical test, it is necessary to make assumptions regarding the simultaneous values of each of the others. Fortunately, we often possess information that enables us to make assumptions such as these, especially in the case of persons we know well. But it does suggest that the study of human behavior is a very complex subject.

THE ANALYTIC AND *A POSTERIORI*

It also suggests that the dispute between rationalism and empiricism may be more complicated than we previously assumed. Empiricists such as Hume, you may recall, restricted *a priori* knowledge to analytical sentences, where sentences are said to be "analytic" when their truth can be ascertained on the basis of deductive reasoning from language alone. We are now in the process of discovering that the language that any specific person happens to employ may be very difficult—perhaps even impossible—to specify with certainty. It therefore looks as though we confront a dilemma, because *a priori* knowledge is supposed to be justifiable independent of experience, yet the only access route available for discovering which sentences are analytic presupposes inferences from experience!

In case it puzzled you at the time, it was for exactly this reason that a "?" appeared in the category for *a posteriori* knowledge with analytic content of Figure 3 in Chapter 7. This discovery hints that Hume's position on the nature of our knowledge of the mind may be even stronger than we previously supposed. Without knowledge of ideas, we cannot distinguish knowledge of relations between ideas from knowledge of matters of fact. Even knowledge of relations between ideas, however, presupposes knowledge of ideas themselves. This tends to suggest, in turn, that even the category of *a priori* knowledge with analytic content only qualifies as *independent of experience* in some theoretically relative, context-dependent sense.

In other words, the class of analytic sentences can only be specified in relation to the grammar and vocabulary of a specific language. The meaning of the words that occur in such a vocabulary, however, may only be ascertained on the basis of inductive inference from public speech and other behavior to the causal processes (strengths of tendencies) producing them. Once conclusions have been drawn as to the meaning of those words in the language under consideration, the class of analytic sentences can be fixed. But if those conclusions are merely the uncertain results of inductive inferences, no firm foundation for drawing the distinction between analytic and *a priori* knowledge and synthetic and *a posteriori* knowledge seems to exist. They appear to be merely two different varieties of *a posteriori* knowledge.

Indeed, from this perspective, the distinction between the analytic and the synthetic appears to be theoretically justifiable in just two ways. One is to retain the distinction as applicable to ordinary language but to qualify its standing as *a priori* knowledge. This kind of "analytic knowledge" can represent the relations between words that are employed by actual language users, but it can never be known with certainty. This is a special kind of *a posteriori* knowledge concerning the linguistic practices of specific persons. It may help to understand an ordinary language, but it can never be completely successful. The knowledge it represents is inductive and uncertain.

The other is to apply the distinction to artificial languages but qualify its status as *a priori* knowledge in a different way. This kind of "analytic knowledge" can represent the relations between words that occur within, say, a language framework, where the properties of this framework can be established merely by *stipulation*. This kind of "analytic knowledge" does not try to capture the relations between words that are employed by actual language users, and it can be known with certainty. It is a special kind of *a priori* knowledge reflecting the consequences of adopting those stipulations. If it helps to understand an ordinary language, it does so incidentally and imperfectly. The kind of knowledge it represents is deductive and certain.

This discussion suggests that the distinctions at issue here correspond to the differences between pure and applied mathematics. The domain of pure mathematics is confined to stipulations and the consequences that follow from them, without any implications concerning the way things are in the physical world. These relationships are purely deductive and therefore can be known with certainty. The domain of applied mathematics, by comparison, extends to properties and relations between objects in the physical world, which are empirical and can only be known with the uncertainty of induction. Thus, the price of deductive certainty appears to be the loss of empirical content, while the price of empirical content seems to be the loss of deductive certainty. No empirical knowledge can be deductively certain.

The relations between higher-level programming languages and lower-level languages can also be illuminated from this point of view. Those who design computing machines must take into account the relationships which are intended to obtain between higher-level languages and the lower-level languages that machines actually execute. Whether a higher-level or even a lower-level language actually functions as it is supposed to function as a vehicle for conveying instructions to a machine, however, requires empirical evidence for its support. Deductive certainty about a program's performance can only be secured at the cost of its significance for actual machines.

COGNITIVE EXPLANATIONS

The conditions that must be satisfied for an explanation to be adequate are similar for scientific explanations in every field of inquiry. Implicitly or explicitly, an explanation has the form of an argument from premises including at least one general law. A description of the event, occurrence, or phenomenon to be explained (the "*explanandum*") must be a deductive or probabilistic consequence of those premises (the "*explanans*"). The law(s) that appear in the explanans must exclude every property whose presence or absence makes no difference to the explanandum as described. The sentences that constitute the explanation—*explanans* and *explanandum*—must be true.

It should come as no surprise that the explanations that

we employ in the ordinary conversations of daily life do not always overtly fulfill the requirements for scientific explanations. This occurs not because there are no laws of commonplace phenomena but because they often do not require explicit mention or are perhaps unknown. If we want to know why the match did not light when we tried to light the fire, being told that it was wet tends to satisfy our curiosity, since we already know—and don't need to be reminded—that wet matches won't light. Such differences reflect pragmatical aspects of specific explanation situations rather than differences in their kind.

A scientific explanation should qualify as a cognitive explanation when some of the factors whose presence or absence made a difference to the explanandum phenomenon are cognitive. The cognitive factors that we have identified in this book include motives, beliefs, ethics, abilities, capabilities, and opportunities, especially those involved in the use of signs. In cases of this kind, scientific explanations for cognitive phenomena are possible only if there are laws of cognition that may be employed as general laws in the explanans of those explanations. As we discovered in Chapter 6 and again in Chapter 7, there appear to be laws of cognition of several different kinds.

An example of a cognitive explanation of a simple kind would involve explaining why John Jones happens to possess a mind of a certain kind M^*. A complete scientific explanation thereof might assume the following form:

(CE-1) General law: $(z)(t)(B^*zt = => M^*zt)$

                                        Explanans

    Specific case: B^*jt1

                ———————————

    Phenomenon: M^*jt1 *Explanandum*

This explanation explains why Jones j has a mind of kind M^* by subsuming Jones' case as an instance of a brain of kind B^*

in relation to a law of form (LC-1), which asserts that every brain of kind B^* has a mind of kind M^*.

An example of a cognitive explanation of another kind might involve explaining why Jones possesses specific semiotic abilities. In this case, a complete scientific explanation may assume the following different form:

(CE-2) General law: $(z)(t)(M^*zt = => (EFzt = u => SAzt'))$

Explanans

   Specific case: M^*jt1 & $EFjt1$

_____ $[u]$

   Phenomenon: $SAjt1'$ Explanandum

This explanation explains why Jones j has symbolic ability of kind SA (say, the ability to speak English) by subsuming Jones' case as an instance of a mind of kind M^*, which could be explained by (CE-1), that was subjected to a history of environmental factors of kind EF (born to English-speaking parents and attended a good grammar school, etc.) in relation to a corresponding law of form (LC-2) (a), which happens to be a deterministic law.

The single line between the explanans and the explanandum of (CE-2) indicates that this explanation has the form of a deductive argument. The deterministic character of the general law invoked here means that an outcome of the kind to be explained occurs as an invariable effect of the conditions specified by the law. The strength of those conditions to bring this outcome about, in other words, is universal u. This, in turn, implies that the nomic expectability $[n]$ for an outcome of this kind is universal $[u]$, too, which means that the logical relationship between this explanans and its explanandum is one of deductive certainty and not inductive uncertainty.

An example of a cognitive explanation of yet another kind might involve explaining why Jones displayed response R. A complete scientific explanation in this case might assume the following probabilistic form:

(CE-3) General law: $(z)(t)(Mzt ==> (Szt = .7 => Rzt'))$
                                                               Explanans

    Specific case: $Mjt1 \ \& \ Sjt1$

$$=================[.7]$$

    Phenomenon: $Rjt1'$ *Explanandum*

This explanation explains why Jones j displayed response R (say, chose to have Rocky Road) by subsuming Jones' case as an instance of a mind state of kind M (including his motives, beliefs, ethics, etc.) that was exposed to a stimulus of kind S (the opportunity to choose between Rocky Road and Heavenly Hash) as an instance of a probabilistic law of the form (LC-3) (b) (Fetzer 1993).

A double line between the explanans and the explanandum of (CE-3) indicates that this explanation has the form of an inductive argument. The probabilistic character of the general law invoked here means that an outcome of the kind to be explained occurs as a probable effect of the conditions specified by the law. The strength of those conditions to bring this outcome about is of the probabilistic strength .7. This, in turn, means that the nomic expectability [n] for an outcome of this kind has the value [.7], which implies that the logical relationship between this explanans and its explanandum is one of inductive uncertainty and not deductive certainty.

The function of these measures of *nomic expectability* turns out to be of considerable theoretical importance. These values reflect the extent to which an event of the kind to be explained could have been predicted under appropriate epistemic conditions. These conditions, therefore, include knowledge of the law and of the specific case to which it would apply (i.e. the explanans, in relation to that explanandum). What these values reflect is the extent to which, within a suitable knowledge context, an occurrence of the kind to be explained could have been predicted. They thus represent the maximum extent to which we might be able to predict human behavior.

FREEDOM AND MORALITY

The prospect of explaining and predicting human behavior by means of laws of cognition raises several fascinating questions. If it is possible in principle to explain and predict the behavior of human beings, then is there no such thing as free will? And if there is no such thing as free will, then is there any point to morality? In particular, what sense does it make to hold persons responsible for their behavior, when all of their behavior is caused? These are very important questions. They deserve to be considered. In the few pages that remain, I shall sketch what appear to be the most important problems that arise at this intersection. But a sketch is all that this can be.

There are three classic positions on free will and moral responsibility. According to the position known as *hard determinism*, causal determinism is incompatible with moral responsibility. The existence of causes for our behavior makes it irrational to hold any of us responsible for our behavior, no matter what our behavior might be. Hard determinists accept the view that all of our behavior is caused (or "determined") and draw the inference that none of us is ever morally responsible for any of our behavior. This is true no matter whether we devote our lives to benefiting others (Mother Teresa comes to mind) or to destroying them (remember Charles Manson?).

The position known as *libertarianism* also maintains that causal determinism is incompatible with moral responsibility. If all our behavior were caused, libertarians would be committed to the view that none of us is ever morally responsible for any of our behavior. The libertarian position, however, diverges from that of hard determinism at this juncture in contending that at least some of our behavior is not *caused*. The existence of behavior that is not caused makes it rational to hold us responsible for at least some of our behavior. Libertarians therefore deny that none of us is ever morally responsible for our behavior. We are responsible when it is not caused.

There are serious reasons for doubting the adequacy of either of these views. The hard determinist position, for example, runs up against the history of legal and judicial practice. It seems to imply that rewards and punishments (praise and blame, etc.) are never appropriate on moral grounds. It strongly suggests that moral standards (codes of conduct, etc.) should not be taken at face value as representing moral values. Even if our laws and court systems perform useful functions, they have nothing to do with morality. In a deterministic universe, it makes no sense to praise or to blame.

The libertarian position, by comparison, runs up against the history of scientific progress. The successful application of scientific methods to one domain after another (physics, chemistry, etc.) strongly supports the view that these same methods can be extended to human behavior (psychology, sociology, etc.). Indeed, it seems very odd to think that people should be responsible for their behavior when it is *not* caused. Doesn't it make more sense to suppose that people should be responsible for their behavior just in case it is caused by them? By their own motives, beliefs, abilities, etc.?

The position known as *soft determinism* attempts to reconcile causal determinism with moral responsibility. This approach accepts the lessons of scientific progress and does not deny that human behavior seems to be caused. It also accepts the lessons of legal and judicial practice by holding that persons often are morally responsible for their behavior even though their behavior is caused. From this point of view, a distinction has to be drawn between behavior that is more or less *voluntary* and behavior that is more or less *involuntary*. What is important about human behavior is not whether it is caused but rather the kind of cause that brings it about.

The soft determinist position does not deny that those who

have certain motives and beliefs tend to behave in more or less predictable ways, depending upon other features of their circumstances. Instead, it takes into account that the influence of various factors of compulsion or constraint may cause us to behave in ways other than those we would have displayed in the absence of their influence. We are *free* in the only appropriate sense when we are able to act in accordance with our own motives, beliefs, ethics, etc. And we are *unfree* in the appropriate sense when we are forced to do things we would not otherwise do because of the influence exerted upon us.

From this point of view, there are significant differences, from a moral point of view, between the behavior we display when we are being subjected to physical violence, threats of harm, and the like, and the behavior we display when we are not. Because the voluntariness of our behavior is amenable to degrees, responsibility for our behavior is amenable to degrees as well. The extent to which we may properly be held responsible for what we do may vary enormously from situations involving external force to others involving mental illness to others involving drug addiction to others involving behavior under duress to others involving more or less voluntary action.

Although the soft determinist position thereby reconciles causal determinism with moral responsibility, the hard determinist and the libertarian could still protest that it makes no sense to hold any persons responsible if *they could not have done otherwise.* Whether or not anyone is ever able to do other than what they have done *under exactly the same conditions* thus becomes an issue of more than passing interest. It is fascinating to realize, therefore, that probabilistic causal tendencies represent situations in which, under exactly the same conditions, more than one kind of behavior is possible. With probabilistic causation, a person really could have done otherwise.

We cannot settle an issue of this magnitude within the brief compass of this book. But it does seem reasonable to adopt a position that holds out the prospect of reconciling the history of legal and judicial practice with the history of scientific progress. Even probabilistic causation is still causation and does not seem to alter the complexion of this debate. It may be worthwhile to observe, moreover, that only one of the four principal motives for punishment (retribution, rehabilitation, removing a threat, and setting an example) seems to be affected by the question of causation. Only retribution appears to be at odds with a belief that human behavior is determined by causation.

The position of soft determinism would seem to be the one that can be harmonized most readily with the existence of a science of cognition. Yet at least one question deserves to be considered before we conclude this introduction. If there are laws of cognition, does that mean that everything we ever do can be systematically explained and predicted? The very idea that whatever we do could have been predicted sounds so depressing that there may be a genuine incentive for *not* studying cognitive science in order to at least preserve the illusion that we really are masters of our own fates! Can nothing be said on behalf of this emotional but nonetheless sincere desire?

It may come as a pleasant surprise that there are at least three reasons for believing that human behavior will never be completely predictable, no matter how much progress cognitive science may attain. The first has to do with the strongest sense of an idea that has figured in our discussion of the nature of signs, namely, the existence of a personal point of view. Personal points of view reflect the cumulative effects of every person's history of causation from their genes to their bodies to their minds to their behavior. Since none of us has exactly the same histories of causation from genes and bodies to minds and behavior, our unique individuality will always endure.

The second has to do with a closely related notion, namely, the transition between thoughts themselves. When we think about something—almost anything will do—we can think about that thing from various points of view. We can think of it as an icon, as an index, or as a symbol. Thinking about it in different ways can cause us to think in turn of other things that resemble things of that kind, that are causes or effects of things of that kind, or that have been habitually associated with things of that kind. Our tendencies to associate one idea with another are undoubtedly affected by our history and all that. They will almost surely always be hard to predict.

Even when our habits of mind reflect high degrees of rationality of belief and our habits of behavior reflect high degrees of rationality of action, our behavior is still not entirely subject to prediction. The motives, beliefs, ethics, abilities, and capabilities that bring our behavior about still stand in causal interaction with our opportunities. So long as the world around us is liable to change, we are open systems whose behavior can be altered by the influence of our specific environment. So long as our powers of observation are limited and our capacity for concentration is finite, we shall continue to be affected by what goes on about us in ways that are difficult to anticipate.

These factors reflect restrictions upon the extent to which our behavior is predictable as a function of limitations on the kinds of knowledge we are likely to ever acquire. In addition to these practical restraints upon the extent to which our behavior can be predicted, there remains the inherent obstacle of probabilistic causation. When behavior is an effect of probabilistic causation, the specific outcomes of particular conditions may be anticipated only with probabilistic confidence. Predictions of responses to individual instances of those specific conditions cannot be known with complete certainty. And circumstances of that very same kind may or may not ever occur again.

The most fascinating issue involving matters of morality, I think, has to do with the origins of morality in criticism. Our capacity for criticism represents an exercise of imagination and conjecture in thinking about how things might be different (how they might be improved upon or be "made better"). Our capacity for criticism—of ourselves, our theories, and our methods—indicates that human minds can contribute to improving their own culture by "bettering" their capacities for communication, cooperation, and community. It hints that, by exercising our higher mental faculties, human beings might contribute to the evolution and survival of our species. Our capacity for criticism could even turn out to be as important as our capacity for rationality.

The perspective developed in this book suggests that the computational conception, which has heretofore dominated research within cognitive science, ultimately cannot be sustained. It thus looks reasonable to predict that future research within this domain will focus increasingly on elaborating the connectionist conception. While the hypothesis of the language of thought suffers from seemingly insuperable objections, the conception of minds as semiotic systems harmonizes with the conception of brains as neural networks. The most promising alternative to the conception of cognition as computation across representations, therefore, would appear to be that of cognition as a causal process involving distributed representations.

FOR FURTHER READING

Those who want to explore these issues further will discover they have a wide variety of choices. The following books are especially recommended for those interested in pursuing points raised in the corresponding chapters.

Chapter 1: Flanagan, O. J., 1984. *The Science of the Mind*. Cambridge, MA: The MIT Press.

A very lucid and well-organized discussion of many of the same figures and problems dealt with here, including Descartes, James, Freud, Skinner, Piaget, artificial intelligence, cognitive science, and sociobiology.

Chapter 2: Care, N. S., and C. Landesman, eds., 1968. *Readings in the Theory of Action*. Bloomington, IN: Indiana University Press.

An excellent collection of papers that approach the problem of explaining human behavior from the perspective of "folk" psychology, it includes an important paper by Hempel that discusses the epistemic inter-dependence of motive and belief ascriptions.

Chapter 3: Searle, J., 1984. *Minds, Brains and Science*. Cambridge, MA: Harvard University Press.

A very gentle but stimulating introduction to many of the issues that we have considered, including the mind-body problem, cognitive science, the structure of action, social science, and the nature of free will.

Chapter 4: Computational: Haugeland, J., 1985. *Artificial Intelligence: The Very Idea*. Cambridge, MA: The MIT Press.

A beautifully written defense of the computational conception that explains the development of this approach from the earliest work on computing machines to recent ideas about automated formal systems.

Representational: Fodor, J. A., 1987. *Psychosemantics*. Cambridge, MA: The MIT Press.

An absorbing if somewhat more difficult analysis of the problem of meaning reflecting a viewpoint that has much in common with mine from one who insists that there still has to be a language of thought.

Chapter 5: Fetzer, J. H., 1990. *Artificial Intelligence: Its Scope and Limits*. Dordrecht, The Netherlands: Kluwer Academic Publishers.

A comprehensive introduction to the theory of minds as semiotic systems, together with a survey of the nature of knowledge, the problem of knowledge representation, and other issues in artificial intelligence.

Chapter 6: Rumelhart, D. E., J. L. McClelland, and the PDP Research Group, 1986. *Parallel Distributed Processing*. Cambridge, MA: The MIT Press.

The original studies that introduced neural networks to the world, whose authors write with clarity and conviction, displaying a remarkable sensitivity to the philosophical issues implicit in their work. (There are *two* volumes!)

Chapter 7: Lumsden, C. R., and E. O. Wilson, 1983. *Promethean Fire: Reflections on the Origin of the Mind*. Cambridge, MA: Harvard University Press.

An utterly absorbing account of human evolution that elaborates the theory of gene-culture coevolution in a fashion that is easily understood, including an introduction to the conception of epigenetic rules.

Chapter 8: Johnson-Laird, P. N., 1988. *The Computer and the Mind.* Cambridge, MA: Harvard University Press.

A very readable and highly informative discussion from a computational perspective, including an analysis of vision, learning, action, memory, reasoning, communication, the conscious and the unconscious, and free will.

Chapter 9: Facione, P. A., D. Scherer, and T. Attig, 1978. *Values and Society: An Introduction to Ethics and Social Philosophy.* Englewood Cliffs, N.J.: Prentice-Hall.

An unusually accessible discussion of issues involving moral responsibility and human values, including problems of self-interest, free will and determinism, rights and duties, justice, society, and conflict resolution.

REFERENCES

Ackermann, R., 1965. *Theories of Knowledge: A Critical Introduction*. New York: McGraw-Hill.

Care, N. S. and C. Landesman, eds., 1968. *Readings in the Theory of Action*. Bloomington, IN: Indiana University Press.

Carnap, R., 1939. *Foundations of Mathematics and Logic*. Chicago: University of Chicago Press.

Churchland, P. M., 1984. *Matter and Consciousness*. Cambridge, MA: The MIT Press.

Cosmides, L., 1985. *Deduction or Darwinian Algorithms? An Explanation of the "Elusive" Content Effect on the Wason Selection Task*. Cambridge, MA: Harvard University Ph.D. Dissertation.

Davies, P., J. H. Fetzer, and T. Foster, 1995. "Logical Reasoning and Domain Specificity", *Biology and Philosophy* 10:1–37.

Dretske, F., 1981. *Knowledge and the Flow of Information*. Cambridge, MA: The MIT Press.

Dretske, F., 1985. "Machines and the Mental." *Proceedings and Addresses of the American Philosophical Association* 59: 23–33.

Dretske, F., 1988. *Explaining Behavior*. Cambridge, MA: The MIT Press.

Edelman, G., 1987. *Neural Darwinism: The Theory of Neuronal Group Selection*. New York: Basic Books.

Fetzer, J. H., 1981. *Scientific Knowledge*. Dordrecht, The Netherlands: D. Reidel.

Fetzer, J. H., 1985. "Science and Sociobiology," in J. H. Fetzer, ed., *Sociobiology and Epistemology*, pp. 217–46. Dordrecht, The Netherlands: D. Reidel.

Fetzer, J. H., 1988. "Signs and Minds: An Introduction to the Theory of Semiotic Systems," in J. H. Fetzer, ed., *Aspects of Artificial Intelligence*, pp. 133–61. Dordrecht, The Netherlands: Kluwer Academic Publishers.

Fetzer, J. H., 1989. "Language and Mentality: Computational, Representational, and Dispositional Conceptions," *Behaviorism* 17: 21–39.

Fetzer, J. H., 1990. *Artificial Intelligence: Its Scope and Limits*. Dordrecht, The Netherlands: Kluwer Academic Publishers.

Fetzer, J. H., 1992. "Connectionism and Cognition: Why Fodor and Pylyshyn are Wrong", in A. Clark and R. Lutz, eds., *Connectionism in Context*, pp. 37–56. Heidelberg: Springer-Verlag.

Fetzer, J. H., 1993. *Philosophy of Science*. New York: Paragon.

Fetzer, J. H., 1994. "Mental Algorithms: Are Minds Computational Systems?", *Pragmatics and Cognition* 2: 1–29.

Fodor, J. A., 1975. *The Language of Thought*. Cambridge, MA: The MIT Press.

Fodor, J. A., 1980. "Methodological Solipsism Considered as a Research Strategy in Cognitive Science," in J. Haugeland, ed., *Mind Design*, pp. 307–38. Cambridge, MA: The MIT Press, 1981.

Fodor, J. A., 1987. *Psychosemantics*. Cambridge, MA: The MIT Press.

Ginsburg, H., and S. Opper, 1969. *Piaget's Theory of Intellectual Development*. Engelwood Cliffs, NJ: Prentice-Hall.

Haugeland, J., 1981. "Semantic Engines: An Introduction to Mind Design," in J. Haugeland, ed., *Mind Design*, pp. 1–34. Cambridge, MA: The MIT Press, 1981.

Haugeland, J., 1985. *Artificial Intelligence: The Very Idea*. Cambridge, MA: The MIT Press.

Hempel, C. G., 1952. *Fundamentals of Concept Formation in Empirical Science*. Chicago: University of Chicago Press.

Hempel, C. G., 1962. "Rational Action," in N. Care and C. Landesman, eds., *Readings in the Theory of Action*, pp. 281–305. Bloomington, IN: Indiana University Press.

Hempel, C. G., 1965. *Aspects of Scientific Explanation*. New York: The Free Press.

Johnson-Laird, P., 1983. "Thinking as a Skill," in J. St. B. Evans, ed., *Thinking and Reasoning: Psychological Approaches*, pp. 164–96. London: Routledge and Kegan Paul.

Johnson-Laird, P. N., 1988. *The Computer and the Mind*. Cambridge, MA: Harvard University Press.

Louch, A. R., 1966. *Explanation and Human Action*. Berkeley, CA: University of California Press.

Lumsden, C. R., and E. O. Wilson, 1981. *Genes, Mind, and Culture*. Cambridge, MA: Harvard University Press.

Lumsden, C. R., and E. O. Wilson, 1983. *Promethean Fire: Reflections on the Origin of Mind.* Cambridge, MA: Harvard University Press.

Michalos, A., 1969. *Principles of Logic.* Englewood Cliffs, NJ: Prentice-Hall.

Newell, A., and H. Simon, 1976. "Computer Science as Empirical Inquiry: Symbols and Search," in J. Haugeland, ed., *Mind Design*, pp. 35–66. Cambridge, MA: The MIT Press, 1981.

Peirce, C. S., 1897. "Logic as Semiotic: The Theory of Signs," in J. Buchler, ed., *Philosophical Writings of Peirce*, pp. 98–119. New York: Dover Publications, 1955.

Peirce, C. S., 1906. "Pragmatism in Retrospect: A Last Formulation," in J. Buchler, ed., *Philosophical Writings of Peirce*, pp. 269–89. New York: Dover Publications, 1955.

Popper, K. R., 1968. *Conjectures and Refutations.* New York: Harper & Row.

Popper, K. R., 1978. "Natural Selection and the Emergence of Mind," *Dialectica* 32: 339–55.

Popper, K. R., 1982. "The Place of Mind in Nature," in R. Q. Elvee, ed., *Mind in Nature*, pp. 31–59. San Francisco: Harper & Row.

Putnam, H., 1961. "Minds and Machines", in S. Hook, ed., *Dimensions of Mind*, pp. 138–164. New York: Collier Books.

Putnam, H., 1981, "Brains in a Vat", in H. Putnam, *Reason, Truth, and History*, pp. 1–21. Cambridge, UK: Cambridge University Press.

Rapaport, W. J., 1988. "Syntactic Semantics: Foundations of Computational Natural-Language Understanding," in J. Fetzer, ed., *Aspects of Artificial Intelligence*, pp. 81–131. Dordrecht, The Netherlands: Kluwer Academic Publishers.

Rumelhart, D. E., J. L. McClelland, and the PDP Research Group, 1986. *Parallel Distributed Processing*. Cambridge, MA: Bradford Book.

Salmon, W. C., 1967. *The Foundations of Scientific Inference*. Pittsburgh, PA: University of Pittsburgh Press.

Searle, J., 1984. *Minds, Brains and Science*. Cambridge, MA: Harvard University Press.

Skinner, B. F., 1953. *Science and Human Behavior*. New York: The Macmillan Company.

Smolensky, P., 1988. "On the Proper Treatment of Connectionism," *Behavioral and Brain Sciences* 11: 1–23.

Turing, A. M., 1950. "Computing Machinery and Intelligence," in E. Feigenbaum and J. Feldman, eds., *Computers and Thought*, pp. 11–35. New York: McGraw-Hill, 1963.

Wason, P. C., 1966. "Reasoning," in B. M. Foss, ed., *New Horizons in Psychology*, pp. 135–51. Harmondsworth, UK: Penguin Books.

Wason, P. C., and P. N. Johnson-Laird, 1972. *The Psychology of Reasoning*. Cambridge, MA: Harvard University Press.

INDEX OF NAMES

INDEX OF SUBJECTS